*"From small and humble begi[...]
celebrate the special people w[...]
lived with purpose and [...]*
— Kevin Vickers, Pastor of All Nations Revival Church

*"As water reflects the face, so a person's heart reflects
the person. Gwen has a heart for God and people. I am
privileged to have her as my friend."*
— Joyce Nuttall, Nurse

*"I liked this book very much; an interesting and enjoyable
read. It is obvious that Gwen has her faith at the forefront
of her writing."*
— Samy Wilson, Nurse

*"From humble home life, adventurous work and darkest
times, Gwen's courage, resilience and compassion sings
of God's kindness and provision. Enjoy!"*
— Andrea Mukhtar, Street Pastor

BITTER SWEET MEMORIES

A Daughter of Wales' Story of
Love, Hope and Adventure

Copyright © 2024 Gwen Wildman

The moral right of the author has been asserted.

Apart from any fair dealing for the purposes of research or private study, or criticism or review, as permitted under Copyright, Design and Patents Act 1998, this publication may only be reproduced, stored or transmitted, in any form or by any means, with prior permission in writing of the publishers, or in any case of the reprographic reproduction in accordance with the terms of licences issued by the Copyright Licensing Agency. Enquiries concerning reproduction outside these terms should be sent to the publishers.

PublishU Ltd

www.PublishU.com

Scripture from the Holy Bible, New International Version®, NIV®.

Copyright © 1973, 1978, 1984, 2011 by Biblica, Inc.™ Used by permission of Zondervan. All rights reserved worldwide.

All rights of this publication are reserved.

Dedication

I dedicate this book to my dad, a true Welshman with music in his blood and poetry in his soul; a self-taught avid reader who, had he had the opportunity of an education, would have written numerous books. To my mam, who despite her disability, raised her brood of singing birds with loving care, mindful that one day they would flee the nest. And to my daughters, Heidi and Tanya, both doctors whose achievements as a medical doctor and PhD are a source of great pride to me. Lastly, to my darling Lorna whose precious life was cut short at age eighteen. Although I cannot see her with my eyes or touch her with my hand, she will always be treasured in my heart.

Thanks and Acknowledgment

More people than I can name have helped me write this book. Firstly, I am indebted to Matt Bird for his support and encouragement throughout this incredible journey – particularly at a stage when I was lacking in confidence. His enthusiasm for PublishU is contagious.

My cohort group at PublishU have also been supportive and I thank them for their constructive suggestions along the way. I eagerly look forward to reading their books.

Two great friends who completed the PublishU writing course and are now authors, namely Kevin Vickers and Samy Wilson. Their individual experiences of what to expect from the course have helped me steer my way through and have been a light on my path. Their published books are an inspirational read.

My daughter Heidi, herself an author and proofreader, has been a great support to me, giving me an incentive to be authentic and encouraging me to fulfil my dreams and to write my memoirs. Tanya my second-born daughter and technophile helped me navigate my way using alternative services to help my grammar – all this during a house move and change of career for her. They are both loved unconditionally and appreciated.

To the "nest of singing birds" siblings – John, Bob, Lewis, Esther, Ieuan and Gwilym – who have all helped fill the memory gaps for me. Each has their own life story but the same beginnings.

To Joyce Nuttall who so graciously offered to critique my manuscript and did so with a fined tooth comb, giving me constructive feedback. I am grateful for her input, especially in remembering detailed accounts of our exploits down memory lane whilst in Kenya.

My friends, Morris and Mary Mclean, who committed more than twenty-three years as missionaries in Guatemala and set up Centro de Enseñanza Biblica in San Luis, El Petén. Now that they have retired and live in Canada, I am grateful to them for updating me with the progress of the Bible College, now renamed "Centro de Educación Biblica."

My Canadian friends, Gerald and Valerie Westcott, who ministered to me in the days following Lorna's death. They are ministering angels and an important part of my story.

To Mair, Mary, Joyce and Beryl – my climbing companions along the ancient footpaths of Wales, Canada and Kenya. They are the spring in my steps and have urged me forward, giving me an extra shove up the hills.

To Erfyl Watkin, a friend and neighbour who now tends the land at Gorsdyfwch, for his help in reigniting my childhood memories. He always kept a welcome in the hillside for my family.

Contents

Introduction

Chapter 1: Bucket List

Chapter 2: Background

Chapter 3: Cleaning Duties

Chapter 4: Uncle Dico

Chapter 5: The Homestead

Chapter 6: Bread, Butter and Jam

Chapter 7: Pig Slaughter and the Cawl

Chapter 8: Home Christening

Chapter 9: Sheep Dipping and Shearing

Chapter 10: Peat Cutting

Chapter 11: School Years

Chapter 12: My First Job

Chapter 13: Nursing

Chapter 14: Midwifery

Chapter 15: The Travelling Bug; South Africa

Chapter 16: Labrador

Chapter 17: Guatemala

Chapter 18: Kenya

GWEN WILDMAN

Chapter 19: Marriage, Children and Career

Chapter 20: Health is Wealth

Chapter 21: Chapel and Faith

Chapter 22: Music and Bereavement

Chapter 23: Welsh Mountain Goats

Chapter 24: Healing Ministry

Chapter 25: Ffald-y-Brenin and Taizé

Chapter 26: Retirement and Christian CARE Merton

Chapter 27: Street Pastors

Chapter 28: Open the Book

Chapter 29: World Day of Prayer

Chapter 30: God of Restoration

Conclusion

About the Author

GWEN WILDMAN

Introduction

Since I retired from nursing, I have felt led and even urged to write my memoirs. An opportunity presented itself when I considered doing a book writing course. I didn't exactly rush into applying but waited to see if this urge was my idea alone or if others could see if there was something of my life story worth writing about. I decided to give it a go, as it would be a learning curve that would be beneficial for me to undertake. I was then made to realise how busy life had become since my retirement, and I had to ask myself why I was cramming so much into "doing" and not just being me. To prepare for the opportune time for writing meant having to give up some of the ministries that I am passionate about namely, "Street Pastors", "Open the Book" and my local charity "Christian Care", to name a few.

I'm writing this during Lent, and I feel it's a journey of self-discovery and discipline for someone active like me who, I've been told, is never still. That's not entirely true as I am often energised to start the day with God's Word and a coffee. I am slowly learning that when we give up our agendas, the place of solitude becomes a place of inner renewal and new insights. As I'm writing, my thoughts about my childhood change, I ask myself if some of the memories were bitter at all, since there was no trauma involved.

As in the inspirational 'Footprints in the Sand' message, one of the reasons for writing down these memories is to leave a footprint of my life through the bitter and dark times and to emphasise that I did not walk it alone but during the hardest times, I was very much aware that I was being carried. I am also aware that as I write, memories can become distorted, so my short-term memory is not as clear as my childhood recollections. I need to share my life story and my faith with the future generation before they get lost in the annals of time. Nowadays having some knowledge of the family history can help healthcare providers identify patterns of inheritance as well as risk factors.

Another compulsion to write is that I am, like Moses, slow of speech. I cannot articulate well and have never mastered the art of public speaking. Even though I do not consider myself a writer, the written word expresses my thoughts more effectively.

Above all, this book is really God's idea.

Chapter 1
Bucket List

As part of the writing course, the group was asked to choose an object or photo as a visual reminder of our primary motivation for writing our book. As writing my memoirs was currently at the top of my bucket list, I chose a bucket.

The dictionary description of the bucket states that it is a deep, cylindrical vessel, usually of metal, plastic, or wood, with a flat bottom and a semicircular carrying handle called a "bail" for collecting, carrying, or holding water, sand, fruit, etc.

On our farm, there was an abundance of buckets in constant daily use, usually aluminium or galvanised steel. The only plastic one that I can remember is a red one that I acquired as a child while building sandcastles on the beach in Barmouth. I treasured this so much, guarding it carefully on the train journey home. Buckets were used to carry water from the spring well at least twice a day; they contained the sheep dipping solution, on washdays carried water from the stream to heat over the fire, acted as a coal scuttle, and carried bits of crumbly peat – the feeding of grain seeds for the poultry and animals. It was the slop bucket for the pigs also containing grain with some of our leftover foods as well. Then we milked the cows morning and evening (which was by hand).

On rare occasions during the school holidays when I did the milking, I still vividly remember some cold winter mornings, helping to herd the cows into the cow stalls. I would sleepily grab the three-legged stool, rest my weary or lazy head on the cow's side and place my bucket firm between my knees, by which time, hopefully, I would be awake. The warmth and the steam from the milk filled the bucket and filled my heart and soul bringing a song to hum along with the rhythmic movements of milking. How it warms my heart as I reminisce about those days! Especially as the cats and kittens would also flock into the cow shed demanding a squirt of fresh milk for their breakfast.

Then there was always a pig swill bucket on the farm. The Ministry of Food advertisement showed the importance of pig swill:

"Because of the pail, the scraps were saved,

Because of the scraps, the pigs were saved,

Because of the pigs, the rations were saved,

Because of the rations the ships were saved,

Because of the ships, the island was saved,

Because of the island, the empire was saved.

All because of the housewife's pail."

BITTERSWEET MEMORIES

This photo is myself as a girl taken by my elder brother Selwyn with his very first camera.

GWEN WILDMAN

Chapter 2
Background

"Memories are timeless treasures of the heart."

Thurman defines memory as, "one of God's great gifts to the human spirit without which neither life nor experience could have any meaning."

"Yng nghesail y moelydd unig" is the way the poet Eifion Wyn describes the valley of Cwm Pennant above Garndolbenmaen in his famous poem.

This roughly translates to, "In the armpit of the lone hillside." For me, it describes "Gorsdyfwch" – the lonely stone dwelling set deep into the crevice of a hillside where I spent my early childhood. The road to the house was rough terrain with a steep hillside.

In his book, 'Madly in All Directions' published in 1967, Wynford Vaughan Thomas describes the scene that greeted him when visiting – in his words, 'the loneliest inhabited place in Wales':

"The hearth remains exactly as it used to be a hundred years ago. A forest of Welsh ham hung overhead from oak beams. A peat fire filled the kitchen with that unbeatable perfume of the open moorlands. The oven beside it added the crisp smell of newly baked bread. A vast iron pot bubbled gently, suspended over the fire. They contained the 'cawl', a stew enriched with leeks and mutton guaranteed to satisfy the appetite of the whole

Jones family in one sitting. Mr. Jones paraded them before us."

My earliest memory takes me back to when my twin brother, Francis, and I were at the crawling stage. Most likely it was the much talked about family conversations concerning this incident that triggered my memory at that time. My mother had placed both of us in the Silver Cross-like pram, unrestrained as was the norm in those days, so that she could get on with her household chores and we would be out of her way. After all, there were always chores for my dad and my uncle Dico, who lived with us both within the household and outside on the farm at Gorsdyfwch.

The story related to my parents is that the pram tipped up with the result that my brother and I both fell out and landed on the hearth. Francis purportedly says that he suffered migraines as a result of a head injury that day – his thorn in the flesh. With no immediate access to medical aid, my parents didn't think there was any concern regarding his health, despite that he vomited but was OK by the next day. Rarely did we see a doctor.

My dad, Dafydd Ellis Jones, would often recount his story of how he, whilst a young boy, came over the hill country from Llangadfan to Gorsdyfwch, together with his mam named Gwen and his sister, Mary. Nain (Grandmother) Gwen had been promised a job as a live-in housekeeper to the owner of Gorsdyfwch known as the 'Gaffer'. Her boss also owned two other neighbouring farms and was quite influential in providing jobs for the local people. Not only was Nain Gwen his housekeeper, but she also went on to give birth to four children with him: Frank, Lewis, Dico and John. According to the census of 1901, the

Gaffer was seventy years old when their youngest son, my uncle John, was born. Subsequently, when the Gaffer died, uncle Lewis and uncle John inherited the prosperous farms. Uncle Frank, by this time, had died on his way back from France during the war and my auntie Mary had left home to get married. Uncle Dico, who was disabled, and my dad were left to rent the impoverished farm and take care of my grandmother. Welsh was the hearth language.

Dad nursed my grandmother through many illnesses and in her last hours he tended to her needs alone. By his accounts, he came back from chapel one Sunday night to find that she had been sitting too near the open peat fire and she had sustained a severe burn to her leg. There was no mention of getting the doctor in those days, it was an expense and besides, there was no money. He took care of her wounds, dressed them with sheets or towelling that was available, and used healing plants from the marshlands. How I wish that I had learned which plants they were! Uncle Dico evidently had seizures in his childhood and didn't have coherent speech. Dad also took care of him as he could, at times, become violent. Little wonder my sister and I became trained nurses.

My mother, Edith Olive lived in one of the neighbouring villages with her seven siblings. She was also disabled due to what I have since discovered to be a congenital stroke – not that the family would notice as she was very active as a mother, wife and carer. Only when she was tired would she walk with a limp and experience weakness in one of her hands. Then she had to use a calliper which she disliked intensely, to aid her walking. This did not stop her from walking miles every week to meet the grocery van, to the local shop two miles away and occasionally meet us from school, particularly when we had forgotten our weatherproofs on a wet day. It invariably rains in Wales.

Mam's close-knit family was well-known in the area. Her father spoke Welsh and, like my dad, was a church Elder. My maternal grandmother was a non-Welsh speaker who soon learned or at least understood the language. Likewise, my mother, with my dad's encouragement soon was, if not eloquent, able to get by in Welsh and communicate with the locals. She also helped dad with his English. This he struggled with as he only had eighteen months of schooling. Mam and her siblings also had only a basic education before they were thrust into working on the farm or were married. I'm not aware of the details of how my parents met. They did not elaborate. I've since discerned that it must have been a wrench for my mother to leave her close-knit family unit together with my stepbrother who was very young at the time to live with my dad and uncle. Neither my dad nor uncle had any experience of caring for a child and Mam and my brother had to cope not only with the isolation but relating to these two men who were by this time set in their ways.

The two-mile walk to meet the school transport was mostly mountainous terrain along a footpath. My father complained to the County Council and requested a paved road otherwise he threatened to not send his children to school. After a lot of discussion, his request was granted. The road was paved but not as far as the farm. When family members visited, which was not very often because of the isolation, they would not risk driving their vehicle down the hill and so would walk the last few steps. My father would then drive them back to their vehicle with the tractor. As children, we walked everywhere until we graduated to bicycles which were always second-hand and were then handed down to the next sibling according to size.

GWEN WILDMAN

Chapter 3
Cleaning Duties

*"Slovenliness is no part of religion.
Cleanliness is indeed next to Godliness."*
– John Wesley

Despite being in relative isolation, generally, there was no fast-paced living – what didn't get done one day or week would get done the next time, the next day or, if it was haymaking, whenever the weather was favourable. As previously mentioned, Mam was never still though, as her work continued all day and well into the evening. As children, we were sent to bed early, sometimes in the summer when it was still light and despite protests, we were encouraged to read until we fell asleep. Most times we would chat. One time, when we would do a quiz with the younger sibling, one of my younger brothers asked the question, "Whose work is never done?" No one got the correct answer except the one who asked the question. Of course, the answer was Mam. Only now do I realise how astute my brother was at the time for one so young.

The only time that we were permitted to have late nights was when we were bringing the hay in and into the barns in the evenings which could be a race especially if the forecast was for rain the next day. Too bad if the next day was a Sunday for no work, except for milking the cows or feeding the animals would be done on the Sabbath. My brothers would look forward to the day when they would be allowed to drive the tractor, the only mechanical implement on the farm. It was quite an event when we had our first tractor, an old Forden which caused great excitement. Previously, our shire horse stallion used to pull the hand plough guided by Dad or uncle Dico to cut the furrows in the fields for planting and later in the year, was used to pull along the hay cutter and rake when it came to gathering the hay.

Although we didn't have a lot of visitors, my parents – Mam especially – kept the place as clean as it was possible. There was the fireplace to clean out and ashes disposed of. Being the eldest girl, the house cleaning such as polishing the grate with black lead and cleaning and polishing the silverware – actually it was cutlery! – fell on me, sometimes reluctantly. I still possess an old-fashioned flat iron similar to the one we had but without the detachable cover base. The iron was heated on the open fire and once the cover was in place, the custom was to spit on it to check if it was hot enough and to add to the smooth shine. That was the best part! The willow-patterned plates on the Welsh dresser were washed and cleaned regularly. My brothers helped with the outside jobs of cleaning the cowshed, kennels and pigsty which all had a back door for access to the large compost pile at the back of the house. All of us took turns feeding the poultry, dogs and pigs and if there was an orphaned newborn lamb, there would be a fight to be the one to care for and feed the Cade lamb (one of the many pleasurable aspects of farming).

Sunday night was a bath and change of clothes night. The bath was an aluminium tub, not unlike the modern ones in which to carry wine and champagne nowadays. The fire was stoked up to heat water continually to fill the bath at intervals. Being the eldest of my siblings, I was almost always the last one to go in which invariably meant the water was not the cleanest and the hot water from the kettle to top up was decidedly not hot.

Why do Mondays stand out in my mind? Well, that was washday, come rain or shine. Mam would start very early in the morning with kettles on the fire continually throughout the day. Hand washing with no gloves was the norm as we didn't have electricity. There would be a bucket of cold water for rinsing before the final blue rinse bucket followed by the infamous mangle. How we loved to have a turn at turning the handle and, despite warnings, often got our fingers squashed in the rollers! There is something satisfying about squeezing clothes flat if only to quicken the process of drying.

The scrubbing board was essential and I'm sure Mam would use this to effect, not only to clean stubborn stains but to express her frustration from the toil and hardship. As children, we would dread coming home particularly if it was a wet day, as clothes were hanging to dry from every ledge with hardly any room to move. If, on the other hand, Mam would be humming a tune, that was an indication that she'd had a good day.

Recently my granddaughter was doing a school project and wanted to know:

1. What was the design of my bedroom when I was a little girl?
2. What programs did I watch on TV?

I was amused but also because I hadn't up to that stage talked about my childhood in any depth, it was an opportunity to share what was perceived as needs and/or necessities. The answers were easy of course: We didn't have wallpaper. We just had a bare stone wall lined with rubble and lime mortar – I shared a bed with my sister and never had a room to myself. TV? No, just a radio. We did not miss what we didn't have.

BITTERSWEET MEMORIES

This is Uncle Dico with (clockwise) Esther, Bob, Gwen, Francis, Lewis and Leuan. Missing from the photo is elder brother Selwyn and younger brother Gwilym.

Chapter 4
Uncle Dico

Uncle Dico was part of my early childhood and as I mentioned earlier, was prone to seizures, presumed to be epilepsy but this was never diagnosed. We hardly ever saw a doctor – only the district nurse who was also a midwife whenever there was a new baby in the household. By now there were seven of us. My elder brother had moved out to work at a neighbouring farm.

I was away doing my nurse training when my parents and siblings moved from Gorsdyfwch to a less isolated stone-dwelling farm called Buarthgerrig (translated as "Stone Bier"). It was not too far from where Francis and I were born, at one of my aunt's dwellings. Mam was the one to insist that the move to access the amenities i.e. shops, doctors and transport to schools would be beneficial for all (especially due to health issues as she and Dad got older). My siblings can still relate to the move as being traumatic, especially for my father who had lived there all his life. There was the sale of all the farm equipment, tractors and trailers (maybe the left-handed peat spads was included). The money from the sale amounted to £200. It was my parents' labour of love but with very little financial rewards.

My siblings still remember vividly a very disturbing incident that has affected them to this day. Shortly after the move, uncle Dico became violent, woke up in the night, and threatened to kill my dad with his stick. It took all of Dad's strength to restrain him by which time all my siblings were fully awake and were trying to help. This resulted in the doctors being called out and my uncle taken to Talgarth which was the nearest hospital specialising in mental health – known locally as the "Asylum". Never will I forget the day I visited him with Dad, Francis and our next brother, Bob. Francis had just acquired his first car and drove the three-hour journey to Talgarth. This visit affected me deeply, not only because it was my first time in a mental health institution but because the whole place signified gloom. It started with a nurse, jangling keys in hand, leading us through several locked-up rooms and finally to Uncle's room. We found him absolutely zonked out (possibly due to medication). He did not relate to my brothers, nor me. He related only to Dad in a stilted and mumbled conversation. Dad was the only one in the past who was thought to understand his rumblings but alas, he could not converse with him this time. So tragic. My sister since this time, had qualified as a nurse, and had worked in Talgarth for a time and ascertained that he had died of pneumonia. The first close family bereavement.

Since reading Dr Enoch's book – 'Enoch's Walk' – it is heartening to know that mental health has changed dramatically since my uncle's time and awareness of many different diseases is more openly discussed.

Since becoming nurses, my sister and I often discuss and try and evaluate the illnesses within the family. We now realise that Mam suffered from post-natal depression probably after the birth of each baby. Being the eldest girl, there was always a baby in the family, so I was the one to help Mam with household chores whilst she breastfed the newborn. I often felt peeved and would feel left out because it was always the baby that got the attention. Was this the bitterness in the back of my young mind? My dad became domesticated, sometimes doing some jobs clumsily during this time, but making sure we were fed and watered. I now realise that it was unusual in that era for men to push a pram or change the baby's nappy, but Dad managed to look after Mam as well and was definitely hands-on. He was never in a hurry or ever seemed stressed with life.

It was no wonder that Mam's health would take time to recover following childbirth. As children we didn't always understand the problems. It was never explained to us, or maybe ill health was not acknowledged. I can only relate to feeling that it must be because of something I've done that my dear mam is withdrawn and not communicating with me or my siblings. Usually, these episodes did not last long but for us as children, it seemed endless. We just longed for the day when she would gain strength and be active again – even scolding us! Slowly she would return to being Mam again and she particularly enjoyed short walks every day and now and again a picnic on the hillside. That was happiness for all the family.

Although quite a bit older than Mam, my dad was a fit man in many ways. Maybe because he was prone to having a siesta in the afternoons! My brothers organised a "sports day" on one occasion and Dad, by this time in his seventies, managed the high jump. We were amazed.

How did my parents cope with childhood ailments? If ever my siblings felt nauseous or eaten something that didn't agree with their delicate stomachs, there would be a saline solution to rinse the mouth or make one vomit. The only medication in the home would be some iron pills for

Mam. Only on one occasion do I remember our local family doctor visit which must have been when my youngest brother was born. It was the district nurse who visited after each child was born. She was a friendly and welcoming presence for Mam coping as she did, not without sacrifices, to care for a household of growing children.

Our isolated dwelling was also mentioned in "Memoirs of District Nurse Evans" when a Nursing Officer accompanied her to experience a day in the life of a district nurse in a rural area. The nursing officer clad in her high-heeled shoes decided she could not continue and quickly bade a hasty retreat. One day Nurse Evans, as she was known, berated our parents for letting us children run around outdoors in bare feet. I don't suppose that we realised the dangers of this or if we had even heard of Mary Jones who had walked twenty-six miles barefoot from Llanfihangel-y-Pennant to Bala to get her own Bible. More of Mary Jones later. Dad used to recycle our Wellington boots to wear as the equivalent of duck shoes by cutting the tops. That also solved the problem of having rash lines on the legs from constant wearing of these boots in the winter. I was very embarrassed when, in the summer my bare legs would be marked by these lines that took a long time to fade. A giveaway for the farm girl who wanted to go dancing!

When my siblings and I got together to talk about how our parents coped with illnesses, there were occasions when they could be viewed as being neglectful when it came to giving the right treatment or getting the medical help that was required. One of my brothers had a discharging ear that was not immediately treated with the result that he now has a hearing deficit. It was my elder brother who called the doctor at the time. To call the doctor required the older siblings or me to cycle forty-five minutes each way to access the telephone kiosk, the only one in the neighbourhood. Many a time, I did this journey with my coins in my pocket, pressed button A too soon before I heard the doctor's voice and lost the coins. It meant a scolding and another journey to repeat the process.

GWEN WILDMAN

Chapter 5
The Homestead

"There is no place like home."

The humble two-bedroomed old stone farmhouse already described, would today be considered uninhabitable. My son-in-law, Paul, when visiting the area for the first time, exclaimed somewhat alarmingly, "But there is only one door! What happens when you have a fire or the chimney catches fire?" Good question and one we would not have considered when we dried our clothes near the open fire, or the wind drew soot onto the living room on a cold day. Coming in from the cold during the winter weather as children we were drawn to the heat and often competed for the nearest place to the fire to warm our backsides when the rest of the room was freezing. Dad was bold to say: "It's a sure sign of snow to come when you warm your backs to the fire." But there was something cosy when we were all huddled together. After all, we did have a roof over our heads.

There was no running water or electricity but, until we started attending school, which entailed an hour's walk, this way of living was considered the norm. At school, however, we discovered that some local families had been hooked up to electricity – even telephones – and there was talk of some having televisions. Now that sounded exciting! There was a natural spring in the back field where we carried water for daily consumption and a small stream from the hillside for washing. The stream tended to dry up in the hot summers but only on one occasion that I remember, did the spring well not produce water. I guess we would have had to walk to the nearest neighbour to get water on that occasion.

Nowadays, this way of living/surviving would sound idyllic in the modern age and some people would long to get away to retreat to such a place. Glamping seems to be the "in thing." Even though we had each other to play and fight with, to me the school holidays were lonely and seemed long and I longed to go back to school with my friends. There were always chores in the house of course and the garden, but a balance of integrating with friends was needed and we often craved company and visitors. Holidays were unheard of; never did we go away as a family. Sometimes during the school holidays, my mam's sister – dear aunt Ivy – would invite two of us to stay with our cousins on her farm. What bliss! The hen coup was converted to a miniature house and the never-ending chatter with my cousins was what comes to mind as I recall those childhood times of make-believe. During our stay, we experienced a real bath which was a massive change from bathing in an aluminium tub in front of the fire at home.

Wynford was right when he observed that there was no sign of money around and everything had the air of being used again and again. Yes, we certainly knew a thing or two about recycling. I am informed by our neighbours that several years ago, our home would have been taken to St Fagan's Natural History Museum as a show house for that Stone Age period, had it not had a new tiled roof that Dad helped to build. Dad, with the help of a neighbour, had also built new hay sheds with an aluminium roof and girders, which, as perceived by us as children, were huge.

It was no mean feat when it was all done by hand. Home for me will always be the place for which I feel the deepest affection, no matter where I am in the world.

GWEN WILDMAN

Chapter 6
Bread, Butter and Jam

The pure comfort foods.

The freshly baked bread. This childhood memory is indelibly etched in my mind with strong memories of comfort, warmth, happiness and family time. It was warmth, especially if I was coming in from the cold. I suspect most people love the smell of bread while it's baking. For us in the West, bread is a staple food and a great source of nutrition in the same way that in other parts of the world, rice would be the equivalent.

There was a lot of hard work and preparation involved before it came to tasting and eating this delicious bread. Did I realise this when I was a girl? Not until I had a family of my own, by which time I had an electric mixer and most of the ingredients within a short distance of the house. However, I have not resorted to having an electric bread maker as the kneading of the dough together with watching the dough rise to twice its size, is itself therapeutic.

From early morning the fire in the grate would be lit with plenty of peat, coal, or logs to heat the oven situated adjacent to the fire. I had no idea how my parents knew when to put the bread in without knowing if the temperature was right. I guess it came with experience. As well as the smell of bread baking, the texture of fresh yeast as it crumbles in your hand, and the sweet tangy smell brings back pleasant memories. The mixing together of the flour, water, and yeast was all done by hand – Dad being the master chef. Depending on the warmth of the living room, and mostly in the summer, the dough could rise in an hour after which the older children could have a go at kneading and claim their bun or loaf by marking their initials on the top.

After the bread? Well, lashings of butter to go on each slice...

Butter Making

At least once a week and twice a week in summer, some days would be allocated to making butter. This took time and energy. Following milking, the milk was left to settle in a shallow dish in the larder where it was always cold. The cream would rise to the top, skimmed off, and put ready for the churn. We had one of the old-fashioned, now antique, barrel butter churns that would turn as well as rotate and as children, we would be expected to take turns in cranking the handle. I cannot recall if there was a specific churning song that we sang to relieve the boredom or aching arms but inevitably it would be a song, a hymn, or something we were practicing for school or a concert. I'm told that the Americans would have several churning songs. "Come butter come, come butter come. Peter stands at the gate, waiting for a buttered cake," being a popular one. On the side of the barrel, there was an outlet and Mam, or Dad, would have to drain the liquid which would be the buttermilk. I associate buttermilk as a refreshing drink, especially in summer days, to quench a thirst.

I often wonder what became of the utensils that we used for butter making. I'm sure that the moulds, spatulas and paddles that were used to knead the butter, would be collectible items today.

After the bread and butter, how about some jam?

Jam Making

We had an orchard with fruit trees – mainly damsons. A little further, about one hundred yards outside the farm, Dad grew potatoes, onions and carrots. But it was the rhubarb that grew best and in abundance. Every summer-season, Mam would be jam-making with rhubarb, damsons and apples and later in the autumn, there would be wimberries. It was invariably our task to go wimberry-picking in the moorlands behind our home and collect enough for Mam to make jam with the amount left after we had scoffed quite a lot of them on the way home. These were idyllic times – the last days of the summer holidays and a look forward to returning to school.

Another culinary delight and a real luxury would be the puddings Mam made with the first milk, heavy with colostrum, from one of the cows after calving. In the first 3 to 5 days of milking the cow, the colostrum is higher in antibodies (so not always recommended for human consumption). My siblings and I are still healthy, very much alive and drawn to this delicacy.

We were never without bread, butter or jam!

GWEN WILDMAN

Chapter 7
Pig Slaughter and the Cawl

Back in the fifties, the slaughter of pigs was governed by the Slaughter of Animals Act 1935, however under Section 2(3) of the Act an exemption was provided for occasional domestic slaughter, which of course covered the average farmer killing the odd pig for family consumption.

As children, we did not look forward to the day when one of our pigs – who had been fattened in readiness – would be slaughtered. Mam and Dad spared us from hearing the screams of the pig and the added anguish of the killing by picking a day when we would be at school. Nevertheless, we were troubled, and we were silent on the way to school knowing that our pet pig would be meat by the time we got home. I would presume that the killing was done by slitting the throat, but I did not ever witness this.

Once the pig was killed, it was drained of blood, the skin scalded to remove the hairs, swilled with hot water and then opened from the throat to the tail and the organs and innards removed. The carcass was hanging in the barn by the time we got home. As we did not have fridges or freezers, much of the meat was later rubbed and salted down with saltpetre on a wooden bench in the pantry which was always cold – summer and winter. It was customary to share the best joints with the kind neighbours who had helped with the slaughtering. I can remember feeling aggrieved that we were left with the salty side bacon bits at the end of the season which had most of the saltpetre in them. Forgetting maybe that in time, we would also be rewarded by getting joints of the best meats from the neighbours.

Mam and the local women had a field day with the remains. Nothing of the pig was wasted. Various dishes were made from the organs and innards. Before the cooking, there would be lots of cleaning of the entrails. I especially like the faggots made with the liver, lungs and heart, mixed with seasoning and bread. My absolute favourite however was the scratchings from the remains of the entrails usually used to make lard, but these were fried for our taste buds and were delicious. Dieticians would not have approved. My brothers and I also enjoyed making a football with the pig's bladder and playing with it for hours until it would eventually burst.

Our pantry was awash with pork for the rest of the year. I'm aware that the constant use of saltpetre was detrimental not only to health. We had to soak the pork joints well before cooking, but the pantry walls would be infiltrated with salt. Not that it mattered to our family then as the stone house was old and would not be habitable for too long in the future.

Today, pork roast is my preferred dish, and bacon pasta bakes a close second.

Looking back to my early days, I am sure that our diet was inadequate for growing children, and we were probably malnourished. Of course, we survived on more than bread and butter, but the diet lacked variety. Breakfast was mainly porridge and cereals when we could afford them. Following breakfast, Mam would put the rice pudding in the oven to be cooked slowly and be ready for midday lunch. Wynford Vaughan Thomas referred to the vast iron pot over the fire bubbling away. This was the main midday meal with enough for supper in the evening. We would have pork and bacon from the slaughtered pig which was included in the cawl but was salty. So why would our canteen lady at our primary school have a quiet word in my ear for my brothers and me to go and see her after the school lunch? Naturally, I thought it was because of some misdemeanour that we had done. But no, the kind lady had put aside second helpings of puddings for us. We thought this was heaven! Most likely we needed more fruit and craved sweet food.

But if we have food and raiment, we will be content with that. I think, though, that my parents sheltered us to the degree that we as children didn't realise that we needed clothing as we grew up and were relatively poor compared to the townies. The nearest neighbour – living the length of two football pitches away – seemed to be equally poor.

From left to right, Esther, Dad, Francis, Lewis, Gwen, Bob and Mam.
Elder brother Selwyn and younger brother Gwilym- not yet born,
is again missing from the photo. Rev. Ap Gerallt is
holding baby Leuan.

Chapter 8
Home Christening

Our local Welsh congregational minister from Carno – Rev W.E. Jones, known to us by his bardic name "Ap Gerallt" – visited our family from time to time and on one occasion, came on horseback to christen one of my brothers in 1954. That made the local paper, The County Times, when we as a family had our photographs taken professionally for the very first time. We all treasured that photograph until it became faded. On another occasion when my twin and I were maybe two years old, we had our photographs taken in a studio in Newtown, a photo I still possess. My dress had a button missing and I looked forlorn and frightened. This time, I realised with a heavy heart that indeed the raiment was lacking and not at all fashionable, but we were content.

Following the home christening, two to three bags full of clothes appeared on our doorstep, complimenting the generous heart of Rev. Jones and his lovely family. What excitement opening the bags and then fighting over items that we so needed e.g. school uniforms! Despite being hand-me-downs, to us, it was nectar from the gods. My sister and I had the best choices of girl's clothes, and we devoured them. I particularly remember getting a green coat which was the colour of the local Crosville buses and I referred to it as my Crosville coat, until it practically fell off me. It was a sad ending and it was too worn to be handed down to my sister, five years younger than I.

The home christening, I realised much later after the event, caused quite a stir in the neighbourhood. With the large heading in the County Times on 9 January 1954, "Where Time Stands Still", the press reporter describes the scene as, "High on the hillside between Carno and Cefncoch time does stand still. Little has changed in the old farmhouse. A radio set to hear the news of the world which is so far away it sometimes seems of little importance. A weekly newspaper to follow the trend of local affairs. A bicycle lamp to cross the farm and find a sick sheep. A Coronation souvenir tea caddy."

You get the drift. Had the reporter been more observant, he would have noticed the birch rod secured under one of the ceiling rafters. When our parents got exasperated with our wild behaviour as we were willed to do, they only had to lift their eyes to the ceiling for us to realise that they could carry out their threat. To my knowledge, the birch was rarely used and never on my sister and me.

It was a bit of a surprise to find this newspaper cutting and discover other's views of how uniquely we lived. We did not know any different. To us this was entirely normal.

Memories are indeed timeless treasures of the heart. When I summarise these memories from childhood, it is the happy times and things of the heart that is prevalent in my mind, like the long summer days of haymaking and being allowed to stay out late to get the haystacks in the barn before the rain came. As in most families, there was sibling rivalry with much fighting as well as make-believe play. Most of this was playing at Eisteddfods but we were a "together" family and eating together was a vital part of communication. Of course, there were challenging wintry days when Jack Frost had been busy designing our bedroom window overnight and Mam was also busy breaking the ice from the buckets of water that we used for our morning wash. By that time she would have got the fire going, but the water in the kettle was not yet heated. Who is going to be brave enough to be the first to surface from our warm beds and face the icy cold flannel on our skins? The wet weather could be frustrating for farmers. Oh! to have the fleece-lined boots and warm parka coats that I wore in Canada (I hope the wool was clean).

GWEN WILDMAN

Chapter 9
Sheep Dipping and Shearing

"He was oppressed, yet when He was afflicted, He didn't open His mouth. As a lamb that is led to the slaughter, and as a sheep that before its shearers is mute, so He didn't open His mouth."
— Isaiah 53:7

Sheep dipping is when farmers immerse sheep in a chemical compound to eliminate scabs, echo parasites, lice and ticks. The sheep on our hillside were dipped in the Spring before lambing time and before ticks appeared. I believe that arsenic-based compounds were used until the 1950s and can remain in soils surrounding old sheep dipping baths. We did not have a dipping bath.

From my childhood memory, the stream and wetlands at the bottom field were blocked off, built up with stones to stop the flow of water to form a small reservoir enough for the sheep to be immersed and plunged into the water one by one. Dad and the neighbouring farmers guided the sheep in for their bath and each one would be plunged into the water. The sheep naturally protested loudly and spluttered when reappearing out of the bath. The dip solution was in a separate bucket and applied to the fleece after the sheep had shaken off the excess water.

Sheep shearing usually followed six months later when the fleece was grown.

The sheep-shearing feast is the setting for Act IV of Shakespeare's play, 'A Winter's Tale.' Thomas Tusser provides doggerel verse for the occasion:

"Wife, make us a dinner, spare flesh neither corne,

Make wafers and cakes, for our sheepe must be shorne,

At sheep shearing neighbors none other thing craue,

but good cheer and welcome, like neighbors to haue."

Shearing day was exciting and one we as children looked forward to eagerly. It was one day in the year when we would have visitors. It was usually held around June or July during the summer months and every year we would yearn for it to be during the school holidays. It was a get-together for the local farmers from the neighbouring farms and, as per rota, each farmer reciprocated by helping each other. My Aunt Ivy would be helping Mam in the kitchen and being the organiser that she was noted for: She would bring homemade cakes, trifles and other delicious desserts in addition to the cawl that Mam had prepared. The desserts and cakes were not something that we had every day, so this day was like having a party. If the shearing day was on a day when we were at school, then we would run most of the mile home and pray that there would be some cake left for us. We were never disappointed, for dear Aunt Ivy had put aside a secret cache for us!

There was a feeling of trust and friendship amongst the men as they had known each other a long time or had gone through life experiences together. I don't remember women taking part in the shearing; only occasionally to wrap up the fleece for weighing and to put it into bags, to clear up the barn after a busy day or, if the shearing was done outdoors, to tidy the yard. The men would oversee gathering the sheep into the fold and catching the next in line to be sheared. The older and experienced shearers would be demonstrating how it's done to the younger men. Most of the time, it looked easy, but until one has handled sheep shears correctly, to shear evenly without cutting the sheep's skin takes a lot of patience and practice. Indeed, it felt like a party, with lots of laughter, teasing and banter amongst them, and we children were onlookers enjoying the entertainment and show.

But it was the women who oversaw the kitchen and served the food. Besides Mam and Aunt Ivy, the local women also joined the throng bringing homemade goodies with them. Bearing in mind that our living room normally housed three adults and five children, it was a bit crowded or what we might describe as being in close fellowship! When all the men had eaten, the women and children would have the second sitting, and again the women would involve us in their conversations and wanted to know what our interests were and if we had any ambitions. We didn't want the day to end. Maybe it was not unlike Shakespeare's 'A Winter's Tale', but to us, it was a feast alright.

GWEN WILDMAN

Chapter 10
Peat Cutting

Sir Winston Churchill's post-war speech struck a chord with me as I'm sure many people wanted to be part of the war effort and country folk were otherwise busy trying to make a living.

"We will be victorious. We will preserve our freedom. And years from now when our freedom is secure and peace reigns, your children and your children's children will say to you, 'What did you do to win the freedom of World War II?' One will say, 'I marched for the eighth Army.' Another will say, 'I was a fighter pilot,' another, 'I was in the submarine service.' And you, in your turn, will say with equal pride and equal right, 'I cut the coal that fuelled the ships, that moved the supplies. That's what I did: I cut the coal.'"

Well, I can say to my grandchildren, "Your great-grandfather cut the peat – that's what he did."

In Wynford Vaughan Thomas' book referred to earlier, he mentions the peat fire.

There was a peat bog on the land where we lived, and it was Dad who in the springtime, with the help of a neighbour, would be seen digging the peat and leaving it to dry. Until recently, I had not realised that peat bogs are vital carbon sinks storing twice as much carbon as all the world's forests combined. Carbons are created when carbon-rich remains of plants are submerged in waterlogged land and turned into peat. Dad once contacted a nature program on the radio and asked why, when digging deep into the peat bog, he found lots of dark wood in the soil. The answer, as our family listened intently to the radio, was that the wood comes from trees that fell thousands of years ago and were buried and preserved in peat bogs. They lay beneath the surface, undisturbed in the acidic bog conditions, until the fens began to be drained.

Dad boasted that he had a unique left-handed peat spade and how I wish I could retrieve it now if only as a reminder of how hard and laborious work it was and the sacrifices it entailed to keep us warm. When the peat was dried sufficiently, it was piled neatly into a cart which was pulled along by a tractor, and the peat was placed neatly again into the barn and stored. It was almost like building a brick wall, but with peat. It was dusty work and tiring. There was no thought about protecting our lungs and wearing masks in those days.

In Scotland's Cairngorm mountains, efforts are underway to restore peat bogs in the name of climate emergency. Also, a recent plan to triple the rate of peatland restoration in Wales will not only combat the climate emergency but protect the curlew of one of the country's most celebrated birds.

Memories are indeed precious treasures of the heart.

Chapter 11
The School Years

"Your childhood is the time of life when God desires to build the rooms of the temple in which He wants to live when you are an adult."

– David A. Seamands

I recall a ritual where my siblings and I gathered around the only table after supper was cleared and sat with the light of a Tilley lamp to do our homework. Now and again the kerosene pressure lamp had to be pumped when the light started to dim.

My twin and I did not start primary school until we were six years old. Dad had very little confidence in the education system. I'm not sure what his reasons were. He purported to have only eighteen months of schooling himself which I assumed he enjoyed, as he related to his schooldays often. He only spoke of one teacher, Miss Hamer, who was very strict and used the cane frequently. Dad, being an avid reader, was self-taught and believed that one can learn from nature and the land. However, Mam and the school authorities, strongly advised him that it would be beneficial for us to learn and integrate with other children, so he relented. We were relieved and so was Mam – already overworked with five younger children in the house. I sensed this was a bone of contention with my parents, particularly when we came home with animated storybooks to read. Dad looked at one of these books with disgust exclaiming, "Talking animals and rabbits with clothes on, whatever next!"

Our primary school had two classrooms. Miss Roberts was the Headmistress and seemed to me to be a permanent fixture in the school (at least during my primary school days). She was dedicated to teaching and highly respected in the community. Not only was she good at her profession, but it seemed to me that she acted as a social worker too. During the holidays, she would invite my brothers and me to afternoon tea. What a treat that was. It wasn't only bread and butter, but jellies and cakes too.

Although I enjoyed my primary education, there was no encouragement to carry on with learning or aim for a career. When it came to taking the eleven-plus before going to secondary school, both Francis and I failed miserably, and this was the start of a downward trend. It meant that we were placed in the B stream throughout the time we were at the grammar and secondary modern school with no extra tuition or encouragement to find out why we didn't excel at certain subjects. With Welsh as our primary language, we were at a disadvantage and struggled with lessons in English. It was generally expected that we were not ambitious and not likely to do anything with our lives except work on the farm. That is exactly what we did.

Chapter 12
My First Job

When Francis and I turned fifteen in July 1961, we didn't return to school and started working away from home. Francis went to a farm in Aberangell earning one pound and twenty shillings and I became a general helper to a family with three children living two miles away with a wage of one pound a week. No equal opportunities then! This was a living-in job and my first time away from home. Although the family adopted me as part of the family and I wanted to get away from the humdrum of daily drudgery and laborious work to earn a living, I didn't belong. They expressed to my parents their concern for me as I was, in their words "painfully shy."

For the first time in my life, I had the luxury and excitement of having a room of my own and so moved in with my meagre belongings: a bagful of clothes, some of my schoolbooks and toiletries. This arable farm was on a much larger scale than our home farm yet was equally hard work. I helped the lady of the house with the housework, cooking, cleaning and caring for the children and when they were in school, there was outside work such as milking and feeding the animals that awaited me.

It was here that I discovered television for the first time. Whatever the family were watching in the evening, I would be glued to the box. My boss was very patient with me but was concerned that I didn't mix with the other youth of my age. However, this was short-lived as I was soon involved with singing, drama groups and folk dancing at the local village. By this time, as I began to earn money, I had graduated from a bicycle to a Vespa scooter and was on my way to becoming independent.

Not long after I moved away from home, my Uncle Dico surprised my employers and me with a visit. It was a surprise because as far as our family knew, he did not communicate clearly to the outside world. As previously mentioned, he had seizures which as children we got used to, and his incoherent speech was just part of who he was. He must have developed a special rapport with us children for in his way, he would defend us by a nodding motion if we were in the right and an exaggerated shaking of the head when we were being naughty. When there was tension between my parents, Uncle retreated to be near us.

My employers could see that I was visibly touched by his visit. I was also embarrassed because of the communication problem. However, he was invited in and had tea with us and then left just as suddenly. It was clear that he missed me and was concerned for me and as I reflected on this incident several years later, I realised that despite not being able to express himself, he instinctively knew a lot more of the neighbourhood than we were led to believe.

A significant event in all my family's lives was Christmas 1962 when I went home for the holidays. On Boxing Day my brothers and I set off to our perspective workplace when it started to snow. This was normal for the winter months but this time it lasted until the end of March and has since been referred to as "The Big Freeze of Sixty Three." I recall drifts as high as the telegraph poles with easy access to the wires that carried high-voltage electrical cables. I was not aware of any potential danger but preferred not to touch the wires as the local farmers had warned us that encountering them could cause electrocution. It was a busy and difficult time as it was the lambing season, and often newborn lambs would be buried with their mothers deep in the drifts. On one occasion, when I was on duty alone watching the sheep for signs of going into labour, I had to call in at the neighbouring farm to get assistance for a breech delivery of a lamb.

Did I realise then, that I would be making a career as a trained midwife several years later?

I was to work with this same family for four years and gained a lot of experience that has benefitted me greatly in my future journey. During this time the owner, realising that farming wasn't in his blood, moved the family (including me) to set up a Merchant Seed Company in Newmills – a complete change for all of us. The children by this time were older and gaining independence and I spent more time outdoors which I loved, especially gardening. There was also the granary work and heaving large sacks to the side for the lorry drivers to place in the lorry. One of the young men helping out with the lifting, tried playing a trick on me one day by catching a mouse and placing it down the back of my neck and waiting for the reaction. He was rewarded with an initial scream and with it, another mouse which I deftly placed down his back. He didn't try that one again!

My working life would have carried on like this had it not been for the local Rector's wife whose name I cannot recall, but who cared enough to ask me what I wanted to do with my life. As I didn't have a dream to aspire to anything, nor a lot of confidence in myself, it didn't occur to me that I was even capable of doing anything else. She invested time with me, asked about my interests and suggested I do nurse training and that she would help with my application. I was mildly interested because a friend of mine had started a two-year course to do her State Enrolled training. "No, my dear," this kind lady retorted, "You aim higher and go for the three-year course and you will become a State Registered Nurse." I am hugely indebted to this wonderful and caring woman who changed the course of my life.

Chapter 13
Nursing

Much like my initial move from home to Wrexham to start Nurse training, I had graduated from a bag hold-all to a suitcase, but still not a lot of material possessions. Still painfully shy, I made friends with those with a similar background and occasionally, and not unkindly, we would be referred to as the "country bumpkins." Again, the townies seemed to be cleverer and more streetwise than my friends and I. It took a long while for me to adjust to the transition from heavy labour on the farm to sitting at a desk. Academically I was not at all confident but made up my mind that, come what may, I would be a nurse one day. If I was struggling, it was going to be the two-year course but on a good day, a State Registered nurse. Even at this stage, there were days when I was still setting my targets too low almost to the point that, like the eleven-plus at school, I was going to fail.

From speaking to relatives on my mother's side, I have learned that my maternal grandmother was a nurse and two of my cousins were working in local hospitals. My grandmother died of cancer in her early forties, and I didn't get to know her except via my aunts who extolled her caring skills and warm nature in contrast to my grandfather who, by all accounts, was very strict.

Graduating from nursing school and becoming a State Registered nurse was indeed a pivotal moment in my life and a phenomenal confidence booster. There were many moments of doubt along the way, hours of despair that I would fail and not be a "good enough" nurse. During these low points, I could almost hear in the recesses of my mind, the Rector's wife urging me onward. Many of my friends felt the same way, having exam nerves and choosing, in the most stressful times, some diversion therapy or switching our focus elsewhere in the form of socialising. In my case, it was taking a walk. The friends I made in nursing school have remained faithful and true companions and we often reminisce about the good old days. We're also thankful that the training at that time afforded us life skills that have remained with us.

The question is frequently asked: Is nursing a career choice or a calling? Clearly, for me, it was a calling from which I made a career. During my time as a student nurse, I specifically remember a patient who was receiving cytotoxic drugs that were making her sick. She said to me, "You're the one that is always here when I need someone to be at hand and you reassure me." This was confirmation to me that I was where I was needed. To have empathy, compassion, patience and sensitivity and to visualise what the other person or patient is going through is surely a life skill in all professions.

My nursing career has allowed me opportunities to specialise in different aspects of caring: from working in an Intensive Care hospital setting, hands-on palliative hospice care, geriatric and mental health to health promotion as a nurse practitioner in a practice nurse setting. I particularly enjoyed my time as a district nurse in South London and got to know the shortcuts when meandering to avoid rush hour traffic when visiting homes. This was holistic care with an emphasis on care for the family as well as the patient. Our District Nurse

Evans did not have to worry about traffic hold-ups in rural Montgomeryshire!

GWEN WILDMAN

Chapter 14
Midwifery

Following my general training, I worked for a short time on a neonatal unit in Shrewsbury Maternity Hospital to await my midwifery training. This was specialised nursing that required skills in dealing with newborn babies and infants with health needs. I was soon to discover that this kind of nursing was more than cuddling cute babies. It required observational skills to be constantly on the alert for any changes or deterioration in the infant's fragile condition. I admired and respected these dedicated neonatal nurses so much. Though I was now a staff nurse, experience and learning had only just begun.

By now I was getting used to tutorial. In any career, the learning never stops. Midwifery training soon came to pass and even though I still found the classroom daunting, overall, I enjoyed nursing mums through their pregnancy and perinatal stages and observing the feeding and caring of the newborn babies. Thinking that helping deliver babies and supporting the mothers was an easy option, I was content to continue this specialised nursing for a longer time, had I not witnessed an emergency Caesarean section which was to test and strengthen my resolve to learn. I was still a student, and in those days, it was rare to find what was later diagnosed as thrombocytopenia in pregnancy. Immune thrombocytopenia (ITP) is an autoimmune condition in which the immune system destroys platelets (blood cells that are needed to clot the blood). This dear lady bled during the operation and neither she nor the baby survived. Such a tragedy. Thankfully more is known now about this treatable condition.

The memorable part of the training was the home deliveries. I have read the 'Call the Midwife' books and subsequently watched part of the series and, as I was now working in South London, could relate to the conditions of that time and know well the area in Poplar where the series is filmed. I can also relate to some realistic dramatic incidences but maybe not quite as gruesome as in the film. Being a farm girl, cycling was second nature to me, but finding my way around the streets of Clapham was a challenge. One day, on my way back to base, I saw my friend and colleague walking her bicycle as she had a puncture. She asked whether I could give her a lift, because she was late for her scheduled visit. I replied that it was no problem. We left the bicycle on the side of the road, she got on my bicycle and whilst she was seated, I pedalled standing upright, and off we went to get to her destination. This was fun and neither of us thought this was out of the ordinary but soon after, we were summoned to the Matron's office where we were sorely reprimanded and reminded that it was unbecoming to see nurses acting frivolously. We were to behave professionally and wear our uniform with pride. Being summoned to the Matron's office was humiliating but I have not forgotten her added words that we belong to a caring profession.

And what of my bicycle? It was still unlocked on the side of the road when I went to retrieve it. The emphasis on professionalism was drummed into us in many of our lectures. We were given a scenario, e.g. If you were in the departure lounge waiting to board a plane and an unkempt, shabbily dressed, unshaven man walks past and you were told he was the pilot, would you fly? We were to wear our uniform with pride and, whilst on duty, always act professionally. When travelling from the hospital to the nurses' home, it was an opportunity to wear the blue wool cape with a red wool lining, tailored impeccably with red straps at the front which kept us warm. If we happened to be on the bus with our capes on, we were given special dispensation and not charged the fare. The public had respect for nurses, teachers, policemen and other caring professionals who were underpaid at that time.

Once a week, I would visit the Chinese laundry with a supply of cotton collars and caps to be cleaned and starched. The nurses got to know the laundry staff very well and they in turn looked forward to our visit. There was an art to folding the cap successfully so that the nurse's hair was neatly in place with none hanging loose. However, the newly starched collars were a menace and many a time would cause rashes on sensitive skin. I think that we eventually got used to wearing the collars or else we developed thick skin, just like the sore feet many nurses experienced from being on their feet or standing for long periods. Those were the days when surgical spirits massaged on our feet worked wonders to toughen the skin, especially when working in the operating theatres.

The nurses' home within the hospital grounds where we lived as student midwives was, after living in various other nurses' accommodations, more like home. Our Home Midwife was our tutor and would organise our rota and occasionally would offer us breakfast before our rounds.

There was lots of de-briefing and sharing with the job and in the home, also time to unwind and relax. In those days it was relatively safe to walk on Clapham Common in the evenings and my friends and I often walked from Clapham South and over the common in search of a restaurant usually following payday. To do this today would not be considered wise.

Often, we would grumble when we've had a busy frustrating day or had to deal with difficulties with staff and patients. It was hard not to compare and admire some of my friends in other professions. On a bad day, we were heard to mumble, "I'll earn more money working in Woolworths or Tesco." Though we did not choose nursing because of the money, we were paid a pittance in comparison to some secretaries in high-powered jobs. Toward the end of the month, I would carefully plan my expenses and there was always a need to cut down on spending or borrow money until payday. That was generally the way we lived.

Whenever one of our family left home to start a career, it was customary for my parents to get in touch through our local chapel minister and connect us with a church with whom we could become part of the church family. My minister communicated with the Reverend O.J. Evans who was minister of the Welsh chapel in Clapham Junction at the time. It was part of their pastoral ministry to care for young people who came to London, look after their spiritual needs and direct them to folks who would befriend them. Indeed, Clapham Junction Chapel had a lively group of young people who met regularly for Sunday worship and Sunday school but also midweek meetings and youth activities with sports and cultural events on Friday evenings. It was a thriving community made possible by Mrs Evans, the minister's wife, who gave of her time and energy to help the young people mature in their faith. Some of these friends still profess a strong faith and will relate to many an incident where Mrs. Evans saw potential in them to become church leaders in the future.

It took me a long time to get used to living in London and finding my way around. As mentioned, my minister had indicated that the Welsh chapel in Clapham was the point of contact for me to attend a service in Welsh and to meet other young people and communicate in our mother tongue. Whilst doing my midwifery training in Clapham South, I was now familiar with the surrounding areas, e.g. I came across a Methodist chapel near Clapham North with a minister whose surname was Jones. I was warmly welcomed into their fellowship but, as it turned out, it wasn't the one that I had been directed to. One day a friend and I walked across Clapham Common shortly after payday and made our way to Clapham Junction where Northcote Road was the in-place to go for market stalls selling affordable produce. It also boasted a historic food market. It was not the yuppie region it is now, attracting young and affluent neighbours but in modern terms, it is still the "in-place."

During one of these visits to the Northcote with another friend, I came across a sign on one of the streets with the inscription, "Welsh Chapel." I literally screamed, not only with delight but relief, that I found what I had been looking for at last. My friend could not understand why I was so emotional about a sign and rightly thought I had completely lost it! Fifty years later, I'm still passionate and still occasionally attend services at Clapham Junction. It is where I met faithful chapel members at a vulnerable time of transitioning to adulthood. They have inspired me over the years to grow in my faith. More importantly, it is the chapel where my husband and I were married in 1973 and where our subsequent children were christened. For a short time, the children attended Sunday school, took part in Nativity plays and concerts and learned a little bit of the Welsh language along the way.

Looking back at my time in the big city, I was anything but streetwise. After all, I was a country girl at heart. After work, on one occasion, I had arranged to meet my friends at a nightclub in the West End. I was living in Streatham at the time and with very little money even for the bus fare, a car with three other men inside stopped and offered me a lift. Without a second thought, I hopped into the car. They were friendly and chatty but then I panicked when I realised that I didn't know them. The car then stopped at traffic lights and in a flash, I uttered that this was as far as I was going and quickly escaped. Shocked to think that I had put myself at such a risk, I made my way back to my lodgings trying to work out why I acted so foolishly. I cringe now as I remember the incident which could have had a very different outcome. There were no mobile phones then, so I could not contact my friends to let them know I would not be joining them. I cannot even remember if I was missed at all.

I surmised later that people were praying for my protection, though I was not aware of this. Shortly afterward I also decided that nightclubs did not have the same appeal.

Chapter 15
The Travelling Bug; South Africa

I suppose my yearning to travel began in my childhood. Having grown up surrounded by brothers, I became a bit of a tomboy to join them in climbing the hillside. Every hill had to be climbed to get a view from the top and there were always places in the distance, other lands maybe, to explore on another day or when we were older. Every summer in early August, we would look forward to our annual Sunday school outing to Aberystwyth and the seaside. Living inland, this was the only time that we saw the sea and I was entranced. There was so much excitement for that day, wondering whether it was ever going to come! Every day I would tick off the date on the calendar, courtesy of H. V. Bowen, the local quarry merchants who supplied the only calendar that I ever remember in our household.

No matter what the weather turned out to be – early August did not always guarantee sunshine – everything about the day was fun: from dipping our toes in the sea, walking into the waves, games on the beach, ice cream and even the shops. Everything was fascinating as it was all new to us. Mam tried to steer us away from the shops, as we had very little money and there were so many tempting things to buy that were way beyond our means. On the way home on the train, I asked Mam who had purchased the delicious ice cream. I don't remember her reply but it must have been a concern of mine at the young age that I was then, to realise we were indeed poverty-stricken.

There was possibly a yearning in me to aim towards a better life in another place where the grass was greener. It was a dream that when I grew up, I could make life better for my hardworking parents and my uncle and earn enough money to support them as they got older. I was able to do this in small measures when I left school and started working but the earnings were a pittance and not conducive to being able to survive let alone save. At the age of twenty, I flew for the very first time to Ireland with some of my nursing friends – it was a first to that lovely Emerald Isle as well. The travel bug within me was aroused and I've never looked back. Nothing quickens my heart as the excitement of walking the steps to board a plane, having a snack and, as we are often reminded, to "enjoy the flight." Those who have a fear of flying would frequently comment that I'm "abnormal"! Quite possibly.

Towards the end of 1969, I was flying again. This time I flew to Johannesburg for a six-month work contract, much to the consternation of my parents who wondered why I was so keen to go and before Christmas! I hadn't given much thought about the right time to go, only that there was a job waiting for me at the Lady Dudley Nursing Home, which in the UK would be called a hospital. There were other British nurses on the same flight that I met for the first time and as a united group, we were ready to show off as well as learn from the experience of working in a different climate and with different groups of people. At the time South Africa was governed by Apartheid – a political system that divided people into racial groups, so alas, we didn't get to come across any mixed races as the Lady Dudley was a whites-only hospital. We were soon to meet many lovely and interesting people but not solely in the hospital. I was to learn and see more of what life was really like for the native people, which was different to the news reports we were exposed to in Britain.

How can I easily forget Florence, a dear hard-working lady who cleaned my apartment and greeted me with a smile each morning? The nurses' residence was situated in Hillbrow – a short distance from the hospital. Hillbrow tower could be seen from my apartment dominating the city skyline. Florence loved to chat and looked through my photo album of my family and shared her dream of one day getting a better job and also wanting an education for her children. One morning she noticed a bag of chips in my wastebasket that I had discarded the previous evening. Without any embarrassment she asked me if she could have them for her children, cold as they were. My heart broke.

I deliberately chose to work night shifts to get time off duty to see as much of this beautiful country in the short time I was there. My Welsh compatriots have friends all over the world so, as soon as news travelled that I was off to South Africa, I was given an address of a family who emigrated from Porthmadog to Boksburg some years earlier. Just a few weeks after my arrival, my friends and I were given a real Welsh croeso (welcome) from the "Roberts", met all their family, had Sunday lunch, and later an introduction to South African "braai." I spent Christmas Day with the family, swimming and enjoying the sunshine and the warmth of their hospitality. The family has now scattered with some living abroad, but I'm still in touch with Gwenda who is now in her nineties. When I corresponded with my parents through letters, they realised that the travel bug would continue for a while longer and they gave their blessing to wherever next I would go.

Through the Roberts, I was introduced to the Cambrian Society which met monthly. Their St David's dinner was a glamorous affair. It was an opportunity to meet both Welsh and Scottish people who had settled into the country but who loved to get together as expatriates to dance and sing. I had the opportunity to attend an Eisteddfod event and was surprised at the high standard of singing and reciting and how competitive the folks were. I met another Welsh couple, Mr Lewis and his wife, who lived in Witwatersrand and have emigrated and made this country their home for many years. They made it their ministry to welcome visitors from overseas, assist them with accommodation and direct them to agencies that would help them settle in. So it was that Mr Lewis arranged for my colleagues and I to have a visit to a gold mine. What a spectacle awaited us as we watched a performance of traditional dances by African mineworkers which preceded the visit underground when we descended deep into the mine to watch them at work. After seeing the cramped conditions that the native Africans laboured with very little light relief, I'm sure these dances helped them let off steam. These miners were exploited by the Apartheid regime and needed to communicate through dance and body language their harrowing conditions letting their Wellington boots do the talking for them as they were forbidden to talk to each other whilst working. I was beginning to learn more about what it was like for the natives to live under such oppression and hardship.

In many ways, I was uninformed about the many customs of living in an African country and what was acceptable behaviour. On the first weekend when off duty, a friend and I took a walk in the local Joburg Park and naively went to sunbathe in a shady spot only to be admonished by the South African police. The police must have realised that we were Brits as they then remarked, "You're not in Hyde Park, you know!" Whether it was the right thing to do or not, my friends and I aimed to do a lot of sightseeing and the only way we could accomplish visiting as many places as possible was to hitchhike.

Looking back, as nurses we could not have done it any other way as we travelled and covered a lot of mileage during off-duty days or nights. One memorable trip was a day's journey from Johannesburg to Oudtshoorn around seven hundred miles, which entailed three different lifts – mostly trucks or 4x4 vehicles. We had stopped briefly in Bloemfontein and were fortunate to then get a lift all the way. Upon arrival in Oudtshoorn, the driver directed us to a local farmer who arranged for us to stay in his converted barn. We did not have the opportunity to see the farmer again as he was up early by morning, already about his business on the farm. To our surprise, this generous man supplied us with fresh eggs, bread, bacon and fresh fruit for our breakfast and directions for the Ostrich farm, our next port of call. This was before the days when the Ostrich farm was the popular tourist attraction that it is today. What kindness.

Another time two of my friends and I wanted to see the sea and we got a lift to Durban on the Eastern coast, famous for its beaches and was known then as the curry capital of South Africa. I remember it was very humid. This time we were offered a lift by an Indian family who were on their way to visit relatives in Durban. They did not seem to think that there was anything unusual for three young girls to hitchhike their way to see the country. We chatted along the way and got to know more about their lives as they too were considered second class citizens and were discriminated by apartheid legislation. They were forcibly moved into Indian townships and had to get permission to enter the Orange Free State Province. These delightful people insisted that we meet their extended family, offered their warmest hospitality and welcomed us to join them in a delicious meal. Yes, the best curry I have tasted! What extraordinary kindness.

One cannot leave this fabulous country without seeing the tourist's top spots: the Kruger National Park was a must. At that time, it was an organised safari tour and well worth the hard-earned money that we managed to save. Without sounding too much like a tourist guide, it was awe-inspiring to visit Pretoria, the infamous Table Mountain, tour the Garden route from Port Elizabeth to Cape Town and from there to the southwestern tip of Africa – Cape Point Nature Reserve. This was a great and unspoiled place to walk with dramatic cliffs and spectacular views. We were led to believe that this was where the two oceans, the Indian and Atlantic, met but I have since realised that Cape Agulhas is the official place.

I loved the people of South Africa so much that I extended my contract for another three months to spend time with them as there was so much more to see. Mair, my Welsh buddy had been working in Zambia and was on her way back to the UK and we had arranged to travel together in the interim, taking in the Victoria Falls and Karina Dam. How did we greet each other when we met? "Livingstone, I presume!"

I returned home full of enthusiasm about my next trip, but I also needed to work and build a portfolio. When I reflect on my time in South Africa, it reads a bit like an extended holiday. In some ways, that was true, but the work could be demanding – especially working in Intensive care and Casualty. Therefore, a balance was needed to be able to have time out from the stresses of critical care. Overall, it was the special people, their welcome, hospitality and generous nature that I have stored and treasured in my heart. I actually came home with the total equivalent of £200 of savings and I thought that I was rich!

GWEN WILDMAN

Chapter 16
Labrador

At a stage in my career when I thought about the future and had a rethink as to what next before I retired, I did what my like-minded friends referred to as "doing a Shirley Valentine." Popular at the time, the film features Shirley – a forty-two year-old Liverpudlian housewife who takes a holiday trip to Greece and meets a local man who bolsters her self-confidence. I didn't particularly want any romantic encounters or discover and rekindle childhood dreams. I wanted simply to experience more of life in all its fullness and have an adventure.

Adventure is what it turned out to be.

I had read about Sir Wilfred Grenfell, a British Medical Missionary, possibly during my nurse training, and how in 1892 he was sent by The Royal National Mission to Deep Sea Fishermen to Newfoundland to improve the plight of coastal inhabitants and fishermen. Tuberculosis and childhood Measles were rife in that part of Newfoundland and Labrador in the 1940s. The Grenfell Mission, which was formed later, helped in eradicating a lot of diseases.

One particular tale and a well-known story about Wilfred Grenfell made an impression on me. In 1908, he was travelling by dog team to attend a medical emergency in a Newfoundland outpost and the snow was beginning to melt. He miraculously managed to get onto an ice-flow with his dogs. As he was drifting on the ice pan without food or water for several days, he had no option but to sacrifice some of his dogs and use their fur to keep warm.

He was eventually rescued by villagers in the area. He then buried his dogs and erected a plaque to commemorate them with the inscription, "Who gave their lives for me."

Grenfell Regional Health Services was formed in 1981 and served the healthcare needs of Northern Newfoundland and the Labrador coast. I espied an advertisement in the Nursing Times that trained nurses were needed to work either in the St Anthony or Goose Bay hospitals or in Outpost clinics. Interviews were to take place in London, and I was soon to meet Nursing Officer Margaret Mahood — a true servant of our Lord and a dedicated nurse. We have become firm friends. During the interview she was ruthlessly honest about the conditions of living and working in coastal communities: the subzero temperatures with long winters, short summers with biting black flies, travelling via skidoo (snowmobile) in winter and coastal boats in the summer. There were no roads between settlements. I was immediately captivated.

I arrived in snowbound St John's on the fifth of November 1989 and stayed in a hotel until the Grenfell medical plane was scheduled to take me to St Anthony. The whole introductory period was exciting as I anticipated meeting other nursing staff in the hospital — some of them with a lot of experience working on the coast and the satellite communities; hearing stories from others. My first nursing station was in Cartwright to do my observational learning with a nurse from Czechoslovakia who had been with Grenfell Regional Health Services (GRHS) for only a year, yet very experienced. I mention this special nurse specifically because we were both on duty on that notable day on the ninth of November 1989 when the

Berlin Wall came down. She had just received a telephone call from her parents with the wonderful news that they could now be reunited with other family members after so many years. It was such an emotional and overwhelming time for her and a privilege for me to be part of this truly historic moment.

Following my induction, I was allocated to work at St Lewis nursing station for the next six weeks as Frances, the nurse in charge, was going back to the UK for a well-earned holiday. She had been working alone for some considerable time and the stress was affecting her health. We worked together well. In actual fact, our Health Supervisors decided that nurses should not work alone. It would help staff retention to work in pairs so that the on-call can be on a rota. Every day was an adventure with Frances. When venturing out of the clinic she would be armed with a kitchen tray to act as a toboggan and whiz down the hill rather than walk on the ice and snow. This became a familiar sight to the amusement of the community folk but, according to Frances, it was safer than falling on the ice and breaking a bone.

I can record so many incidences but there is one big event that both Frances and I will always remember:

Frances was on-call this particular night and she had a call before midnight from a lady in early labour which in her case, was twenty eight weeks and the lady was expecting twins. Frances woke me up as she needed help because the birth was imminent. I groggily got out of my warm bed and went immediately to work getting the incubator warmed and ready for the baby. Meanwhile, Frances the midwife had already been on the phone and arranged for a team of midwives and paediatricians from

St Anthony Hospital to medivac and transport mum and babies to the hospital. Whilst waiting for the medivac team and plane, Frances delivered a premature baby who was placed lovingly in the incubator. It was in the early hours as the dawn broke that the plane finally arrived, and mum had not delivered the second baby yet. As the team took over, Frances and I made cups of tea for the family members who had congregated in the clinic rejoicing with the family that one baby was alive and at the same time anxious about the second twin. Twin two was later delivered safely in the plane when over the Straits of Bell Isle. It was a memorable night and the outcome was good in that the twins are now grown up and healthy.

I did relief duties to cover holidays in various clinics in Southeast Labrador and northern Newfoundland. This proved a worthwhile experience as each community was unique and the people welcoming. One elderly gentleman asked me where I had come from and when I replied that I was British, exclaimed with surprise that he was honoured that a nurse would travel so many miles to come and visit him in his humble home in Labrador. He welcomed me warmly and enthusiastically. Invariably the nurses were asked the same question which I thought rather sad, "How long are you going to be with us?" It seemed that there was a problem retaining staff to work in remote areas as many became stressed, especially working long stretches without a break. If the weather was "down", meaning there was fog or poor visibility preventing planes from flying and if we had a patient waiting to be medevac'd, he or she would need to be nursed day and night until the weather cleared. Sleep deprivation was common among staff in busy clinics. Our supervisors would ensure that we were given time out regularly to prevent burnouts. The Grenfell Regional Health services provided accommodation at St Anthony hospital for coastal nursing to chill (pardon the pun).

Many special occurrences that I can only describe as phenomenal happened to me whilst in Labrador. I was called out in the early hours of the morning to an elderly gentleman who was having, what his daughter states, were panic attacks and she was worried. I cannot exactly remember the real reason for the call; only that, having called the maintenance man to fetch me, I grabbed my medical pack, anticipating all sorts of illnesses, making quick diagnosis in my head all the way to the patients' house. It turned out to be OK. Whatever the outcome, I advised the family to bring their father to the clinic for blood work the next day. All was well at that point. The phenomenon? It was one of those rare magical nights; the glistening snow, the moonlit night, there were mesmerising northern lights, or aurora borealis; it seemed that the stars were dancing in the stillness of the night. And to think I missed it on my way to the patient! But I surely felt it on my way back. Heavenly! Pure magic. It was a reminder of the concern we have for the patient, for each other, and whether we have missed anything in our diagnosis etc. These burdens we can carry in our hearts, yet we also need to offload. Once I had the assurance that the patient was well, I could fully enjoy the moment.

In every nursing station I worked in, there was Grenfell's "footprints" in the archives. In Mary's Harbour, there was an old pump organ just like the one we had in the parlour at home. I was immediately transported to my childhood and our Sunday evening singalongs after chapel. I could imagine Dr Grenfell on the hospital boats or floating clinic, visiting each nursing station and arranging a service where he would welcome the opportunity to preach the gospel. According to the elderly inhabitants of the community, it was customary to sing hymns well into the night when he visited. Labradorians love music and most of the people I met were, like myself, self-taught. Some especially were very good at playing the accordion despite not reading music.

A Christmas-time tradition known as mummering or janneying was not unlike the Welsh Calennig (New Year's gift) when we as children would go farm to farm to sing and/or recite and wish the farmers and their families a happy and prosperous new year. We would then be rewarded by a juice drink and a cake and if the farmers asked us for an encore, that deserved another cake. The mummers in Labrador who dressed in disguise also involved singing, but also dancing and reciting poetry during the twelve days of Christmas. The hosts had to guess the mummers' identities before offering them food or drink. Only when the mummers have been identified, did they remove their disguise and spend time with the hosts.

The little Anglican Church in St Lewis was fortunate to have a minster and his family who were resident in the community. I saw the church and the nursing station as an extension of our service to the community when considering holistic care. Rev Steve Laskey and the nurses at the clinic worked well together and often referred patients to our respective ministries and we would visit each other to unwind for moral and spiritual support. Having a resident minister ensured that there would be a weekly service when the weather allowed. Steve spent a lot of his time travelling to the other communities, either by skidoo in winter or in his boat in the summer. On my first day attending a service, I was asked if I would like to play the organ. I was aghast that the folks would ask me – someone who does not play, neither read music, but improvises – to lead and play the hymns. But in a way I could identify with the ones who, like me, enjoy singing God's praises and making music from the heart and not from the book. I think Dr Grenfell would have been pleased with our communal effort at the church and also at those nursing stations who still had the pedal organs.

There are lots of highlights when I look back at my time on the Labrador coast, living and working in the communities with people that resembled my way of living simply – sometimes so that others can simply live. I could relate to carrying water from the wells, hanging washing on the line and baking bread. However, skiing, snow shoeing, snowmobiling and taking part in the winter games was different as was salmon fishing, visiting satellite communities and summer cabins. It did seem strange to me that a family who lived in the isolated communities would choose to get away to their cabin in the woods which was far more isolated. It was their way of chilling out which, I'm sure we can all relate to. Being an outdoor person, I especially enjoyed skiing which was a real stress reliever. I was not too keen on accompanying the fishermen on their boats to check the salmon nets. They were obviously masters at their job, and I admired them but couldn't wait to see land before the seasickness took hold.

On one occasion in January, one of the young visiting doctors who was holding clinics for the weekend and myself decided to do some cross-country skiing from Port Hope Simpson to the next community, Charlottetown – around thirty kilometres. It happened to be the coldest day of January and taking the windshield factor into consideration, the temperature was well below minus. Skiing across the frozen ponds was biting cold and we thought that we were suitably clad, but I developed frostbite on my ear as a result of a tiny hole in my hood. My young companion started off enthusiastically but became silent as we progressed. We stopped off at different shelters along the way and tried to get a fire going with the kindling that was left for starting a fire and eat our lunch, but our hands were numb with the cold. We had communicated with friends in Charlottetown that if we were not back before dark, to come and rescue us. What a relief to see in the distance the light of the snowmobile of our rescuers with warm drinks and extra clothing. On hindsight it was not the wisest thing to have done, given that we could have come across hungry black bears on the way. Maybe it was a good thing that we didn't light a fire. We certainly got a name for ourselves, never quite lived it down and got teased mercilessly. But what an adventure!

My time in southeast Labrador was also a faith journey and I slowly took on the role equivalent of a Lay Reader. I was soon to learn more about the Anglican Church of Canada during my time in St Lewis and Port Hope Simpson, arranging services when there was no visiting clergy. I got to know the church families and preparing the young people for church membership was sheer delight. This was a course I was asked to undertake especially if the minister was travelling to other communities and in between. There was a newly built café where I met with four young people as part of the course and they just loved the opportunity to talk – not just about their faith but as we got to know each other they would divulge their innermost concerns and their dreams for the future. When it came to discussing the meaning of the Eucharist, as it was referred to in Canada, I invited them to the clinic kitchen to make bread together. After kneading and putting into pans, and whilst we waited for the dough to rise, we discussed the story of Passover and the unleavened bread before placing the bread in the oven to bake. When it came to sharing and eating the fresh bread, I asked these friends how they felt. One said that she was looking forward to being confirmed and for the visiting Bishop, when he came, to give her bread and wine. Another said that she had observed her mother making bread and she was now going to give it a go and whether we could please do it again. It was obvious that we had all received a blessing that day.

GWEN WILDMAN

Chapter 17
Guatemala

In 1993 whilst in Labrador, I took extended leave to join Global Outreach Prince of Peace corps to volunteer for ten weeks in Guatemala. Other than hearing about the Guatemala Civil war of 1960, the Earthquake of 1976 and some epic volcanoes that were still active, my knowledge of that country was minimal. I soon learnt about the ancient Mayan ruins and bustling markets during my short visit.

What drew me though, was the Potter's House in Guatemala City and what was then known as the Dump Ministry. This endeavour started soon after the devastating earthquake that destroyed so many homes and nearly 1.5 million people were left homeless. One Christmas, two young Guatemalan ladies felt called to supply blankets, warm drinks and a Christmas message to homeless young people and children in Guatemala City. This was a very courageous act of kindness, as women, following the political violence on women and gender issues of the early nineteen eighties were quite vulnerable, and the city was not altogether a safe place. Fundraising in this male-dominated area also had its challenges. This act of kindness which started small as a mustard seed has now grown into a large ministry and still exists today.

These two committed ladies, realising that there was a great need to help the homeless, went on despite the difficulties to fundraise and later purchased a building or shack in which to expand this project. It was very much akin to the basic put-up shacks that the locals in the area built for themselves. When I visited this building, offering to volunteer at the clinic that was set up, it was buzzing with people, and the queues outside seemed never ending. It was a privilege to work with an American missionary doctor, a pharmacist who distributed the medicines, a translator and Amy who was soon to start her nurse training. This was a great opportunity to practice the extra skills like suturing wounds, set up an intravenous infusion and try to bandage wounds of the heart as well as the physical wounds. The premises also grew with added buildings to house a canteen offering daily meals, another area with clean water, washing and showering facilities and clothes. During the time I was there, we were involved in making crafts with the women, helping them with ideas to create something out of their collections that they had scavenged from the dump that day. I witnessed them making small purses, bookmarks and belts – items which they could easily sell at the markets.

These women had a hard life of destitution trying to make a living and they longed for a better future. One lady said to me that Potter's House had saved her life. She related how she had contemplated suicide when she felt worthless and could not envision a future for herself. By coming to Potter's House, she felt held and listened to. She admitted to having a faith but through hearing the gospel preached as well as applying Christianity in acts of loving service, she recommitted her life and later joined the staff at Potter's House. The women were industrious and quick to learn. I was showing one teenager how to knit and within an hour of practicing, she had mastered the knit stitch. I was flabbergasted. From the stories that these girls shared with me, I also sensed that some of them had been abused and mistreated. Due to unemployment and other problems, alcoholism was rife in some homes.

My most memorable day in Guatemala City was when I accompanied a medical doctor who had a private clinic in the city and in her spare time, she ministered to the "Dump" people i.e. the homeless who lived on the streets. What an eye opener. The doctor was well known to the street people so she was often followed and she in turn would ask them how so-and-so was getting along and if he (they were mainly men), was adhering to the treatment from last week. It amazed me how the doctor was able to distinguish one shack from another, but she instinctively was familiar with the territory. One incident is indelibly etched in my brain. My nose smelt this noxious aroma long before we entered this particular home. As in the other homes, the family greeted us warmly especially the doctor whom they related to with ease. This doctor was also their "saviour", she spoke their language and listened. The foul smell came from a pot boiling on the stove in their one room abode and was none other than another fowl − a vulture (probably one of many who encircled the dump every day). Whilst we may recoil and think of contamination and the toxic effect of eating vultures, this family was probably starved and risked eating it just to survive.

As this very interesting and exhilarating day came to an end, I was intrigued and asked the doctor which of the ministries gave her the most job satisfaction. She enjoyed working at the private clinic of course and there were vast differences between the clients, the gap between rich and poor was very wide. The homes even contrasted greatly. Even though the working people attending the private sector had great needs too, the difference between the two contrasting groups of people was that she felt a call to use her skills to help the poor. It was a joy to meet this dedicated doctor whom I shall never forget, and I thank God that she heeded that call.

To begin at the beginning, the journey began with some training days in Buffalo where I met students and young people who were bound for different locations around the globe. Most were on short term contracts prior to deciding what their calling was. Two American whizz kids, Teri and Amy, were to be my companions destined to El Petén in the northern part of Guatemala. Teri, a teacher, was a proficient Spanish speaker and Amy was soon to begin her nurse training. How I was to reap enormous benefits from both of them during our time in El Petén! Our hosts were Morris and Mary McLean, Canadian missionaries with Global Outreach with a vision to build a Bible School in the area. What dedication and what an example of obedience and total commitment to that vision! Already they had immersed themselves in the community, had learnt the language and formed a support team. With the help of friends in the community, they had built a very basic dwelling for themselves. Suddenly all five of us were crammed into this tiny dwelling with compartments of rooms and bunk beds for us – the guests – for eight weeks, a real endurance test. Without electricity, I was full of admiration for the way that our hosts were able to dish up delicious one-pot meals using a camping stove.

To get to our destination, M&M, as they were lovingly referred to, had driven nine hours from Guatemala City to San Luis, El Petén. The first four hours were spent along highways but the last step of the journey was along very rough terrain: sometimes muddy and now and again the road had been washed away. It was hot and humid as the Petén rainforests were not far away geographically via the jungle route. In the first week, we all helped to grace the local church with a fresh coat of paint, a great way to get to know the people and learn the local language. I made sure that Teri was not too far away to translate for me. We found that the humidity sapped up our energy, so occasionally we would have a siesta, as the locals did, to conserve some stamina for the evening. It seemed that a lot of insects and animals would come alive at night, and it could be extremely noisy, probably preceding the heavy rains that we heard almost every night. In the morning, because of the rain, there were fresh avocados that had fallen off the trees and were just waiting to be picked for breakfast. Luscious and not a bit like the ones we buy in the shops in Britain!

Vocational Bible School was new to me as was working with children, but not to my American friends. We had activities for the children to engage in, plenty of singing, drama and storytelling. To see how the children get so engrossed in the story was thrilling to watch, interactive and fun. When it came to singing the alphabet together with words to rhyme with each letter, my American friends insisted on the last letter being "zee" whereas I would say "zed." The local church services were quite lively and nearly every night there would be preachers who would belt out their sermons via a loudspeaker in their local dialect to compete with the other nocturnal noises.

Looking back, besides the experiences gained from my time at the Dump, it was working alongside children that gave me the most satisfaction and fun. Never would I have envisioned that thirty years later, I would be involved with Open the Book (OtB) and sharing Bible stories with primary school children which is also interactive and a lot of fun.

Chapter 18
Kenya

Since my time in South Africa, there was a strong urge to go back to Africa when I retired from work. The opportunity came with the arrival of a Pastor from Kenya from the World Council of churches to work at our local Methodist church. For many travellers, Kenya is one of those "bucket list" experiences for visiting nomadic Maasai villagers, climbing Mount Kenya, going on an exciting safari, guided nature walks and bush meals. Some of these were on my agenda, but the main reason was to use my nursing skills and volunteer to help in various clinics in Magina and Kijabe.

Our church organised several trips to this beautiful country: the first in August 2005 to the subtropical highland climate of Baraimu in Meru and to the much cooler weather in Magina in 2007. Among the highlights, we visited Kenya Methodist University and learned that in 1956, the Methodist Mission approached the Meru County Council and requested allotted land. Their request was granted, and they were allotted fifty acres of land where they established the Methodist Training Institute in 1958. This institute grew over the years and merged with two other colleges to become "The Kenya Methodist University." As Methodists, this was of special interest to us.

Following our trip to Magina, I went alone to volunteer and found myself immersed in the local community visiting schools, feeding programmes, women's fellowship groups and HIV groups. One of the highlights was the weekly Bible study at the Jambo Sana Centre which was set up in Magina. Kijabe was the nearest Mission hospital, eight kilometres from Magina. The local African inland church pastor and his wife kindly offered me accommodation that was convenient for hospital visits and not too far from the J.S. Centre and from where I was invited to the local primary school to teach lessons in hygiene and health every week. Imagine my surprise on my first morning at the school when I was asked to lead the morning assembly and the whole school – around two hundred children – congregated in the schoolyard! Without any PA system, it was a real challenge for me to make myself heard and understood and a bigger challenge for the pupils to get a good glimpse of me even standing on a makeshift chair. I'm sure the children enjoyed the entertainment even if they didn't understand the accent. Being the only white person in this particular area, I was often the object of curiosity and intrigue.

From small beginnings (yet Zechariah 4:10 says, "Who dares despise the day of small things?"), the interdenominational Bible study started in September 2007 and grew to overflowing. It was a chance to get to know these young people, some of whom were very familiar and had a reverence for the Word of God. They had learnt the Scriptures from childhood and enjoyed the fellowship and the lively discussions. I was concerned that a lot of the youngsters, when asked what their ambition in life was, wanted to be a pastor. Was this a way to earn money and get out of the poverty trap? More concerning was that they did not possess a Bible of their own in their mother language.

Through fundraising via my local Ecumenical committee, the Mary Jones walk and some individual giving, Vicky, Joyce and I spent a memorable and exhausting day wading through the Nairobi traffic to get a matatu to Kasanari. We were collecting one hundred and thirty-six Bibles from the Bible League office armed with a suitcase and a backpack each. When we saw the bulky load, we quickly realised that there was no way the three of us could manage to carry them. We made tentative plans to return for the two boxes remaining. As we were pondering this, a bishop from Sudan came into the office and was on his way to Nairobi by car and fortunately for us, gave us a lift as far as the matatu stop for Kijabe. The matatu touts wanted to charge us for the extra seat that our load occupied but soon relented when we explained that we were carrying Bibles. It was a real joy, therefore, to present Bibles to the young people and two pastors in our group who were key leaders in the community. The group had completed a ten-week study course and were now wanting to set up their own Bible study. That's growth.

Whilst in Magina, I was often asked why, as a "muzungu" ("white person") I did not make use of the car that was available for my use if needed. Usually my reply, besides the rising price of petrol, was that I would miss the fun of the matatu experience and identify with the local way of life as well as do a little to help with the environment. Besides, the walk from Magina to Kijabe reminded me of the rough terrain and steep hillside of my homestead. On occasions when I needed the car to carry heavy loads, a few extra bodies would suddenly appear in the back seats assuming a lift. One day Joyce, Monica and I with five little children in the back, had not estimated the extra mileage we had done by going along rough terrain and we consequently ran out of petrol along a used highway on our way back. Monica then hopped onto a matatu to go to the nearest petrol station whilst Joyce and I amused the children with games and singing songs. It was getting dark, and we later confessed to each other that we feared for the children's and our safety, praying that Monica would also be protected.

The children however were having such fun with these muzungus, and we admitted that the praise songs kept us focused. We were relieved when Monica returned with another of our friends and with petrol. Kenyans are very resourceful when it comes to make do with what's available in an emergency. Within minutes, we used a coffee filter, made a hole in the base to make an excellent funnel for pouring petrol into the empty tank, and were soon back on the road. That day was memorable as, looking back, it had started with a flat battery in the car, then no petrol. Later in the day, all three of our mobile phones needed charging and so did my camera. But this was Kenya, and I would not trade the experience.

It was at one of these Bible studies at the end of December 2007, that the post-election violence broke out. I could feel the tension all around as our young people were constantly messaging each other on their mobile phones as they scanned the news. When the election results were finally announced, there was a mass exodus from our centre to the highways. Watching the news following the violence was heartbreaking, especially the worst hit areas of the clashes: the massacres at a church in Eldoret and the displaced in Kisumu. Our friends in Magina and Kijabe had relatives living in the troubled area who had to flee their homes and consequently lost their businesses. Everyone around us seems to have been affected by the violence in one way or another.

I was unable to fulfil one of my ambitions to climb Mount Kenya before my return home, as the planned trip was cancelled due to the crisis, shortage of petrol and road blockades. Although I was disappointed, I had the opportunity to join the African Inland Mission in distributing food, clothing and medical supplies and ministered to the displaced families in Maai Mahui, nestled at the bottom of the Rift Valley. We discovered that a lot of Kikuyus people feared to go out as they were one of the tribes targeted.

December being circumcision month in Kijabe, I was invited to an initiation celebration service. Through the African Inland Church, the young men when they reach the age of fourteen, have a week during which they are taught the biblical principles relating to circumcision and learn of the cultural and ethnic reason for the procedure. The programme also included teaching from a doctor who explained the procedure, taught them HIV awareness and to show respect to women. A trained counsellor was available to answer any questions. After a week of being cared and catered for and camping in the local church hall, it was no surprise that many did not want to go back home, feigning that their wounds were not yet healed!

I mentioned mobile phones earlier. Yes, towards the end of my time in Kenya I had seen what a difference having a mobile phone had meant for businesses, especially if companies wanted to contract work at short notice. Safari was heard constantly on the radios, advertising and purporting to make good deals at low prices. I'm sure that by now, more companies are competing in this technological field. I recalled a time when I first visited Kimende with a friend and usually, we would get a Matatu back to Kijabe as we didn't want to travel when it got dark at around six and seven o'clock in the evening. Invariably there would be a hospital transport vehicle around the same time, transporting nursing staff to the hospital for their night shift. It was always a pleasure and a relief to get a lift back to Kijabe with them. The drivers got to look out for us, we enjoyed the chitchat with the nurses and the banter between us. The scene was very different when I returned in 2009 when almost all on the hospital transport were engaged in chitchat, but on their mobiles.

Back to buckets...

Buckets were also a necessary part of daily living for the people of Kenya. During my time in Kijabe in 2007, there were families whose children, before their school day started, regularly walked a mile along rough terrain to the nearest stream and used buckets to fill their water carriers for the journey home. Many locals had cisterns and hand-dug wells with buckets that were dropped by a rope into the water forty meters below and then cranked up. Having experienced, during my time with these lovely African people, how much stamina is required to pull on the rope and then lift the bucket, I have such admiration for their dedication. Hopefully, I have learnt a lot from their simple way of surviving.

My prayer for them would be that "water would flow from their buckets; their seed will have abundant water" (Numbers 24:7).

To put things in a proper perspective: What a comfort to know that the combined might of earthly nations is next to nothing – a drop in the bucket or a speck of dust when compared to God's power and dominion! The King of all Creation who can pick up the whole earth as though it were a grain of sand, is indeed powerful (Isaiah 40:15).

GWEN WILDMAN

Chapter 19
Marriage, Children and Career

Following my adventures in Johannesburg, I returned to the UK but found it difficult to settle in jobs. I joined a nursing agency to see what was available to fill the gap, to earn a living, and to put my skills to good use. Along with two other friends, I had applied for work in Texas which, according to the advertisement, promised opportunities galore for British nurses and a chance to experience the American dream. Alas, this was not to be. Through the London agency, I purposely requested jobs that offered accommodation so that I didn't have to depend on friends who offered me a place to stay temporarily. I wanted to be independent. At the Nelson Hospital, I was offered work on the gynaecological ward and loved it. Little did I realise then that this would be the place in South London where I was to spend most of my work and thereafter my retired life.

My life was to change from then on because there I was to meet Roy who would become my future husband. His mother was a patient in the ward and introduced me to her son. Maybe she wanted a nurse in the family, but I got to know the family well over time: After we married, we lived with my in-laws until we got a house of our own. Roy was an only son and our backgrounds were very different, especially when it came to sharing. It was a difficult and devastating time for both of us when we came to the decision to end our marriage despite many attempts to reconcile. After all, we had both made promises to God witnessed by our families, to love each other. I choose to dwell on the good things that happened, especially being blessed by three wonderful children, a lovely home and my fulfilment as a mum. To quote Michelle Obama, "a beautiful and challenging balancing act", I can look back and be thankful that despite the hardships, we all – my husband, children and myself – survived the challenges that were to come, relatively unscathed.

Most young girls, at least in my days, had illusions of meeting the handsome man of their dreams, having their own house and having children to love and nurture. Just sometimes, some girls would aim to have a professional career and make something of themselves. That wasn't top of the list for me as I achieved most of my aspirations through marriage, home, and children and thought I could retire! It was my husband who encouraged me to pursue my nursing career for my benefit as well as to have an outlet from the domestic routine. Life was busy and on a different scale to my upbringing where there was no electricity or modern conveniences. Despite having a moderate lifestyle living in the London suburbs and having all the essential home equipment and labour-saving devices, there didn't seem enough hours in the day to achieve my goals. So, going back to nursing allowed me to focus on caring and was a distraction energising me to balance a healthy family life.

Like my dad, my husband was a good parent and a hands-on father who took great delight in the children's upbringing and was involved in their education; nurturing and disciplining them. Just like children are a gift from God, so they have been a great blessing to their father (Psalm 127:3). What a responsibility. As parents, we were both hands-on, balancing family and working life to make it work. When I read Henri Nouwen's, "The Return of the Prodigal", I was reminded that God is both mother as well as father. In Rembrandt's painting, God the Father touches the son with a masculine hand to hold and a feminine hand to caress. Children need both hands.

"Can a woman forget her baby at the breast, feel no pity for the child she has borne? Even if these were to forget, I shall not forget you. Look, I have engraved you on the palms of My hands." This verse from Isaiah was a constant reminder for me in subsequent years when following a painful divorce – my children and I became separated. This is when I started a journal, or writing blogs to coin a modern phrase, to help me record my thoughts and feelings on paper. It was a period of self-discovery, and in time, I could get to understand what triggers negativity so I could avoid those and concentrate on being positive. This journal is proof that my children were always on my mind and in my heart whilst we were apart one from another.

God brings beauty out of ashes as the words of the song, 'Beauty for Brokenness' by Graham Kendrick conveys,

Beauty for brokenness,

hope for despair,

Lord, in your suffering world

this is our prayer.

Bread for the children,

justice, joy, peace,

sunrise to sunset,

your kingdom increase!

God of the poor,

friend of the weak,

give us compassion we pray;

melt our cold hearts,

let tears fall like rain;

come, change our love

from a spark to a flame.

Like a bereavement, the stages of denial, anger, depression and acceptance following the breakup of a marriage are very real.

"Suffering is not a question that demands an answer; it's not a problem that demands a solution. It's a mystery that demands a Presence." – Anon

It was during my time working with the Grenfell Regional Health Services in Labrador that I received a call from my, by this time, estranged husband that was to further change the course of my life. Having been working in Labrador for almost five years, I was on my way home but had planned a holiday to see my friends in Nova Scotia. Samy, one of my colleagues working in another nursing station on the coast of Labrador, informed me that Roy was trying to get hold of me and that she had given him the number to contact me. I happened to be relieving for holidays in another nursing station that weekend and recall feeling a sense of foreboding when she told me this, because it was very rare, if ever, for Roy to ring me at work.

When I did receive that oh-so-memorable phone call, it was with unbelief and total shock that I struggled to take it all in. After the initial reaction of my letting Roy know that I did not want it to be true, he literally bellowed down the phone that indeed our lovely daughter Lorna had been involved in an accident and was dead. He felt at the time that he had to be brutal in saying this bluntly as I was probably in total denial. As I mentioned, I felt unbelief initially but afterwards, I felt an indescribable calmness that Lorna was in a safe place. Where did these thoughts come from? Of course, grief then set in and my dear friends who ministered to me said that I was curled up in a foetal position on the couch in the days that followed and whenever they visited. Samy and the local community then arranged for other colleagues to stay with me. This was the caring and nurturing nature of GRHS and Wilfred Grenfell's legacy that when one of God's children suffers, we all feel the pain. Margaret Mahood, my wonderful nursing officer and friend who was in charge of the coastal nurses, arranged a flight home for me in a first class with another nurse to accompany me and who was also on his way back to the UK.

During the days, months and times of grieving that followed, I could relate to the words of Gee Taylor whose son Anthony was murdered in 2005 when she asked, "How do you mend a broken heart?" Anthony was the same age as Lorna when they died. The sense of being utterly broken is real. Each one of our family would go through the stages of grief differently and in their own time. I was reminded that Roy and I had a life before we had children, but for our daughters, Lorna had been part of their lives.

Chapter 20
Health is Wealth

I have been blessed with good health most of my life. Unlike my twin who has endured migraines for most of his life until recently, rarely do I remember being sick as a child with the odd exception of contracting Chicken Pox. Conveniently, all my siblings and myself were affected with this childhood illness at the same time and we stayed off school. Never was Mam so relieved than when we recovered.

When I was diagnosed with breast cancer in 2005, my initial reaction was a calmness which later became an inconvenience! I was still working and making plans for retirement with so much to accomplish before my last day at work. It could not have happened at a worse time. Actually, it was exactly the right time.

I'm not going to pretend that the chemotherapy and the radiotherapy that followed were pleasant. There were days when I felt lousy, depressed and out of sorts. The day that I could not bear the ice cap that was to help preserve my head of hair any longer, I broke down because it was so uncomfortable. But it was the discerning, caring kindness of the nurse in attendance that made my tears flow. She understood and empathised.

I do now see this cancer as a gift. The time away from work allowed me to take stock and reassess my life and activities and I was found wanting. Even though I remained fit by swimming, jogging and cycling, a lot of evenings were taken up with meetings etc. This all took a toll on both my physical and mental health. In between treatment slots, I was fortunate to enrol in a computer course. When I was first diagnosed, one of my friends, being a staunch evangelical minister, suggested I go for faith healing so that I would not have to go through the planned treatment of the Oncology team. When I had completed and was reviewing the whole period of my treatment with my friend, I said to her that, if I had taken her advice, I would have missed countless blessings – the doctors, nurses, hospital staff and the patients. It was different being on the receiving end of the nurses as a patient; there was no nurse/patient barrier. As patients, we could identify with each other and I could pray with the other patients when called to. What a privilege that was.

To summarise, 2004 was a year full of events. It was a long and difficult journey at times, but also full of blessings: the crown and cross, joy and adversity, sunshine and rain and many contrasting words that come to mind, like dawn after a long night, song after pain. The year was indeed bittersweet for me.

I had no idea that the breast cancer treatment would take so long: almost nine months. Remembering the most difficult times, especially the darkest valley of chemotherapy, it was only when I looked back that I realised how weak the human body is to counteract these drugs which are poisonous to the body and sometimes to the spirit, and I have appreciated this only after having been restored to full health.

What about the blessings? They are more than I can count, being surrounded by the care and love of my family, the kindness of my neighbours and work colleagues, the doctors and nurses, and the friendship of my fellow patients. I was able to empathise with my fellow patients much more and feel closer to them because I was in the same condition as them and this was a lesson for me as a nurse.

As part of the aftercare, we were offered complementary therapies at The Haven Clinic in Fulham and one day, by chance, I came across this sacred Haven. I went to see what the clinic had to offer and was overwhelmed by their loving care both individually and as a group exercise or therapy. From the beginning, I felt a bond with the place. The decorated circular rose-stained glass window in one of the upstairs rooms exuded light and life. No surprise then when I found out that the building was where Walham Green Welsh Chapel used to be. Many of my friends who were members of the chapel can testify that it had the best congregational singing in London. I gazed at a column stone laid by Timothy Davies on 7 June 1900 and imagined the spirit-filled services, the powerful sermons and enthusiastic singing of the past. Though it is no longer a chapel, this Haven continues to serve those in practical or spiritual need through the prayers of the faithful saints of the past ingrained in the walls of the building.

The NHS Long term plan for cancer states that "after treatment, the person will move to a follow-up pathway that suits their needs and ensures that they can get rapid access to clinical support." I have to admit that Oncology was a branch of medicine that I did not specialise in and I was soon to discover that the aftercare dealing with the effects of chemotherapy and radiotherapy was excellent and there was plenty of information booklets available. We were encouraged to work towards promoting healthy lifestyles; regular physical exercises, adequate sleep and avoiding unhealthy activities like smoking or excess stress.

I well remember the day when I decided I would no longer wear the NHS wig that I wore for the most of my aftercare. It had served me well, particularly in keeping my head warm and boosting my confidence at the time. It was a source of hilarity when my family took a photo of me sitting in the garden with the wig draped over my face, and when my son-in-law Paul performed a skit of the pantomime dame. But the wig hid the real me. One Sunday morning, I was the church steward on duty, welcoming everyone to the service and introducing the visiting preacher. It gave me a much greater confidence booster and a sense of empowerment when I accomplished this "just as I am" mode without the wig. The new hair growth that was beginning to appear signified progress that I was on my way to wellness.

Health is wealth indeed.

Chapter 21
Chapel and Faith

"Goodness and Mercy (God's sheepdogs) will follow me all the days of my life"
(Psalm 23:6).

From the time that I started walking, it was natural for myself and our family to go to chapel, at least twice on a Sunday and occasionally, when we were invited to tea, three times. Often my younger siblings would be carried on our parents' backs. Some of these walks during the night were quite magical, especially when we witnessed glow worms on the way. As children, we were fascinated by their glow. My brothers decided on one occasion to pick one up and carry the beetle home in a matchbox but once it was touched, it no longer glowed. Alas, the matchbox was empty when they arrived home. How disappointing, but it was a lesson for us not to interfere with nature.

Only on special anniversary services would we go to church as a family. It was deemed necessary to always have a person manning the farm at all times. Dad, being a staunch Independent Congregational Elder, would often go to a midweek prayer meeting or an Elder's meeting. Mum belonged to a local Methodist church that her parents were acquainted with. The two chapels were equal distance from home, i.e. a two-mile walk each way and offered us the opportunity of either going with Mam to the Methodist or with Dad to the Independents. There was a lively Sunday school in both chapels for us as children and for different age groups. As we got older, we could even join the adult classes. That was a promotion! There was no difference in the order of service and the congregation was welcoming and child-friendly in both venues. Maybe it was worth going to the chapel to get the sweeties as a reward for saying a verse from the Bible every week.

On very few occasions, maybe when there was no school the following day, I was allowed to accompany Dad to the midweek prayer meeting which was a very different experience for me the first time I went as a teenager. For a start, it was mostly men that led the meeting. Besides my dad, my Uncle John and other local farmers would each kneel and pray sometimes loudly and with fervour and passion. I remember feeling uncomfortable, embarrassed and terrified through not knowing what was going on. This was not the dad I was accustomed to at home. Not until much later did I learn that these men were products of the 1904–1905 Welsh revival, when illiterate people who were full of the spirit of prayer could soar loudly and in refined language. Dad who was around nine years old at the time, often referred to those days with relish as he would hear stories of lives that were changed as related to by his mother. The revival hymns were the ones he chose at these meetings.

The memories I have of those early days were having to endure long and boring sermons. Learning a verse every week and having to stand up to recite them to the congregation from the "set fawr" ("the big seat") was nerve-racking at times, but nearly always there was an elder nearby who would whisper the verse to me if there was a time of stage fright or that I had forgotten the words. The Big Seat is where the church ministers and the elders would be seated – usually facing the congregation. Almost making them separate from the common people but in those days, as children, we would be expected to give them the utmost respect. Nevertheless, I'm so glad that a lot of churches that I am involved in presently, do not have that seating separation. Often the lectern is on the same level, so there is no craning the neck and getting a "pain in the neck" from constantly looking up to the pulpit.

We would not expect children today to endure listening to a sermon of even five to ten minutes unless it was peppered with activities and visual displays, and I thank God that we can do church differently now where adults and children can be involved. Godly play, Messy church and Bubble church are just examples.

Godly Play UK is a Christian movement centred on childhood spirituality. Godly Play promotes open and creative ways to explore Christian story and practices, so the art of using spiritual language meaningfully can be enjoyed by families. Messy Church is a way of being church for families and others. It is Christ-centred, for all ages, based on creativity, hospitality and celebration, helping families to grow together in their walk of faith, and not see Christianity as something you grow out of at a certain age. Bubble Church is a Sunday church service especially for babies, toddlers and young families. It's a puppet-packed, Jesus-centred, coffee-and-croissant-fuelled, thirty-minute kids and family adventure.

When I remember these snippets of chapel life now, it is the family times together, the walks and chatter along the way and the excitement of seeing friends and neighbours that come to mind. Most of all, and without realising it at the time, I have memorised a lot of Bible verses that were hidden in the recesses of my mind. How else would I have answered my dad when still a toddler all those years ago? When he asked me if I had put enough polish on his shoes to make them shine, I answered "'Yn glaer wynion", without realising its implication. This was a hymn using words from Isaiah 1:18, "Though your sins be as scarlet, they will be as white as snow." I was not aware of all this until I overheard Dad having a conversation with a neighbour and implying that out of the mouth of babes will come wisdom and that he was proud of his children. Wow!

Although my parents loved us all deeply, there was no outward expression demonstrated and I have since observed that this was normal for a lot of families back then. I don't recall Mum and Dad praising us in front of our neighbours or in our hearing. On the contrary, there were cries of "do better next time." Other than holding hands and embracing us when we were hurt, there was no peck on the cheek or kissing unless it was to "kiss it better." Besides the love and care that my parents showered us with, there were no observances of faith rituals in the home; Mum and Dad read the Bible but there was no grace before meals, nor daily devotional time for the family. It was only the hymn singing on Sunday nights. By then, we children were so exhausted from Sundays – the busiest day of the week. Something of those days, especially the words of hymns, are permanently etched in my mind. They come back to me as answers to prayers or when worried about family or friends in distress.

Even though I can say that I had a Christian upbringing of going to church regularly, I cannot say I was a committed Christian. That process took time and God, even in my childhood, was already nudging and guiding me to experience more of Him in my life. There were times when I was challenged, especially by the words to the hymns that we sang that reminded me where my destiny lay but I was not taking heed at that time of my life. Although as a toddler, God had His hand on me, I did not understand the verse that came out of my mouth. Up to that stage of my life, I didn't realise that, if I was willing and obedient to His will, He could make me clean and white as snow.

One of my nursing colleagues in Labrador used to do a lot of night shifts when her children were small. She often related to me how a certain gentleman patient once told her that he had difficulty sleeping and added, "Please don't tell me to count sheep because I've tried that!" She advised him, "Try talking to the Shepherd." It was many years later when a chance meeting between my friend and this same gentleman took place and he was pleased to let her know that he had been talking to the Shepherd ever since.

Our sheepdogs on the farm were well trained and very loyal to their masters, often relating to the male members of the family more than Mam, my sister and me. Maybe the females in our family could also be likened to the sheepdogs that follow at the rear of a herd. Goodness and mercy are similar to sheepdogs guarding a herd who walk shoulder to shoulder watching out for us and protecting from the pitfalls in our own lives. It is the Lord who is the Good Shepherd.

It was July 1989, when Billy Graham came to Wembley stadium and many of our local churches were organising buses for groups to attend and we were encouraged to bring a friend. I remember that we were a motley crew of all ages on the bus, some with faith and others none, but all singing together. There was great excitement for the journey ride through the London traffic anticipating a great evening. I cannot remember much of Pastor Graham's message, but only that I was, to quote Charles Wesley, lost in wonder, love and praise. The singing was heavenly, and I was carried to the seventh heaven of bliss. I persuaded my two friends to accompany me for the altar call, but they needed no persuasion and so we were drawn like magnets and directed to a ministry team. All three of us were challenged in different ways, to live a life worthy of the calling that we had received as Christians. My faith journey started to change and mature from that moment on.

Ever since my move to London, I have been a member of The Presbyterian Church of Wales, first in Clapham Junction church where I was married and where my children were christened. The Welsh Presbyterian church in Sutton is now part of the United Welsh churches in South London and has become my spiritual home for the past twenty-five years. There is absolutely nothing that excites me more as worshipping God in my native language and the thrill of communicating with those in our small congregation who long for an opportunity to converse in Welsh, even if it's just once a week.

I am currently a member of my local church at Martin Way Methodist, but no longer as active as I would like to be. Naturally, I miss the fellowship. Serving people requires a sacrifice of time that I am no longer able to give. I will always be grateful for the opportunity to be able to serve in a variety of ways throughout the years, including the choirs, Street Pastor training, Home Groups and Churches-Together committees.

As Chapel secretary and Elder at the Presbyterian Church of Wales in Sutton, I am now spending more of my ministry time pastoring the members in outreach projects. Before the pandemic, our minister met with the elders to discuss the future of the church, as the building needed a lot of maintenance. The elderly and dwindling congregation was unable to meet this demand and it was a source of great worry. We made this a matter of prayer. During the pandemic, when we could not meet at the church, we formed a WhatsApp group and met weekly on Zoom for fellowship. This turned out to be a real blessing for the house-bound members and those who were no longer able to attend worship. As one member said to me, "We see more of each other now than we did when attending church."

The Chapel has seen answers to prayer since we started the weekly prayer meetings following the pandemic. We have been blessed by a young and vibrant youth mission enabler working alongside our Minister Richard Brunt and all the Welsh Chapels in London. Also, since partnering with Suttonfx and reaching out to the local community, it has been such a joy to meet and get to know many who live locally and have Welsh connections. Suttonfx was established in 2021 as a lay-led church initiative working in central Sutton. This initiative is committed to creating and running projects that bring church and community together.

The Welsh Chapel in Lind Road, Sutton was originally built as a Primitive Methodist chapel and is listed in Kelly's 1891 Directory as holding services on Sundays at 11:00, 15:00 and 18:30. The Surrey History Centre holds records, accounts and a baptismal register for this church spanning from 1917 to 1963.

From that time until today, the building is now a place of worship for a Welsh Presbyterian congregation with services in the Welsh language. The architect of the chapel is believed to be William Wilmer Pocock (1813–1899). He started working for his father in 1837. He was one of the first students at King's College, London and graduated from the University of London. In 1861 he designed the Metropolitan Tabernacle at Newington Butts. In 1875 he designed the Central Chapel of the Welsh Methodist in Hastings and in 1878 the Chapel, School and Soldiers' Home in Aldershot. He died on 18 September 1899 and is commemorated in a stained-glass window in London's Wesley Chapel.

Chapter 22
Music and Bereavement

To quote again from Wynford Vaughan Thomas' book:

"'The children all produced mouth organs and proceeded to give us a selection of Welsh folk songs.' 'A nest of singing birds, that's what we are,' said Mr Jones with pride, 'And I'm a bit of a poet as well. So, what do we want with television and the rest of that stuff.'"

You may wonder why I chose to include music with bereavement as a chapter heading. According to scholars, music has been proven to be effective in managing emotional and physical symptoms by decreasing the perception of pain and increasing physical comfort and relaxation.

Music featured largely in our home and in school. Whatever was sung at school assembly would be repeated ad-nauseam all the way home and in the evening. Someone in the family would be humming a tune whilst cleaning teeth or whatever job they were doing. Anyhow, there would always be items to practice for concerts or eisteddfods. In the parlour was a pedal organ or harmonium, where Dad as a chapel organist would practice the hymns for Sunday and as a family, we would gather on a Sunday evening after chapel to sing. All our family had mouth organs and learned to pick up tunes as none of us could read the old music notations; only sol-fa. When at school, we had lessons on the recorder and we were encouraged to sight-read.

Recently a friend of mine, Sioned, daughter of Reverend W.E. Jones (mentioned earlier) shared with me how she had learnt music using the tonic sol-fa through my father. By her accounts, he was an imposing figure with his tuning fork in hand and taught a class of Sunday school children the Curwen modulator. This was the method used in our primary school and, according to my brother Francis, most of the members of the male voices choir that he belonged to were sol-fa literate. Every Good Friday, our local chapel had an eisteddfod. As children the competition was fierce, especially between the local schools. My moment of glory from those days came when I won first prize in the Modulator competition (most families in the area were competitive and were, to my mind, competent in music with proper degrees to their names). This confirmed to me that I have an ear for music and will often revert to the sol-fa method.

Did we realise the significance of singing together and how therapeutic, in my case, it has proven to be? It's such a shame that singing together in school programs are now a thing of the past. However, during my school years, it helped to build confidence; much like choirs and community singing are not self-focused, but rather on listening to other voices and being part of the whole. Like my dad, I often play the organ to lead singing at my local chapel but like to sing as well as play. So, I prefer to change the word "playing" to "improvising."

In 2018, as part of our pastoral duties, my friend and I was visiting two of our church members at a local care home, both of whom were in the dementia unit. Sometimes when the conversation became stilted or non-existent, we would hum a tune. Invariably some of the residents would stir and start reacting to certain songs and often, before we left, it would end up as a singsong for everyone in the room. As we were encouraged as a church to reach out to the community, we went back to a small group in the church who loved to sing, formed a singing group and started visiting the dementia unit every week. As we got to know each resident and their families, we also could discern who the singers were. Spreading ourselves amongst the residents to form a circle and sitting holding hands or tapping out music was beneficial. Once the session began, the songs became spontaneous. If one of the residents started mouthing or humming a tune, then we would join in. It was sheer joy to have the carers join in and request the hymns that mean a lot to them. Often when we would have a cup of tea afterward, it was a thrill when residents would start singing again and was an affirmation that we were indeed making a difference.

I have learned valuable lessons along the way, which has been humbling. My nursing career and experience do not mean that I am an expert in dementia care – far from it. Many a time I have had to stop myself from saying, "Do you remember?" A memory deficit affects most of the residents and only makes them feel agitated to be reminded of something that was long forgotten. As I've got to know something of their history, there would be songs that would be familiar to them, i.e. the ladies that have been in church choirs would not be comfortable singing the drinking songs. Also, as we are part of the church ministry, we are sharing our faith in praise with those who may not have heard the gospel message. What an opportunity we have.

Since music was and is an integral part of who I am, it did not surprise me that during the saddest and most troublesome times of my life, it was the orchestra within me that was in my brain and came to the forefront of my mind at the right time and allowed me to express what was in my heart. A piece of music could lift my spirits or allow tears of sorrow to well up inside. I experienced times of grief where it was impossible, besides the groaning, to pray. However, I knew that others were praying for me. Words of hymns from the inner recesses of my brain would suddenly come to my mind as if in answer to my prayers.

At least three indescribable occurrences come to mind when I try to remember these significant and tragic events in my life. I have already mentioned that on being given the dreadful news that Lorna had died, I experienced an inner calmness which could not have been explained in natural terms. This was before the inevitable shock and grief had set in. The second occasion was at Roy's funeral. Our daughters and the closest family members were gathered at the church vestry to have prayers with the officiating minister before the service. As soon as the minister started praying, I felt this overwhelming and overpowering sense of peace wash over me.

The year 2005 is when I had the third surprise and I had what is commonly called nowadays a health scare through being given a diagnosis of breast cancer. My initial reaction to the news was anything but scary. I asked myself whether this was normal.

But I sensed yet again that peace that passes all human understanding which took over and came to the forefront of my mind.

How do you explain this to your family or the secular world?

The events surrounding Lorna's death were still painful to recall and they often bring back memories that surface at unexpected moments. It is possible that some of those memories were hidden until I could cope adequately and confront my emotions. However, I will not easily forget the time when an angel came to minister to me as the family and I were preparing for the funeral. Roy had contacted the local church of Scotland's minister beforehand so that we could discuss an order of service together. I had just flown back from Canada and was still grief-stricken as well as jet lagged. All family members cope with grief differently: my daughters, husband and extended family were no exceptions. This dear minister, whose name from memory was "Morag", discerned immediately after we met that I had no one with whom to offload my feelings and offered me a room and hospitality at her manse. This was the ministering angel that came at the right time and gave me space, rest and her counsel if and when I needed it. I can relate that I encountered angels unawares that day.

How does one cope after a sudden death and bereavement? Some parts of the funeral service passed in a blur in the memory. During my quiet time in the sanctuary of the manse, those comforting words of promise from Paul's letter to the Romans came flooding into my soul. "Nothing can separate us from God's love, not even death." Those were familiar words for me, but their meaning was never as real as in that moment. Many purport to become busy, to immerse themselves in their jobs and keep moving. I did all of this and more – especially talking to friends who had time to listen and who would let the tears flow. I thank God for them. There was, however, no comparison to being able to join the fellowship of believers that gathered at church and letting myself be real before God. Again, it was the words of the hymns or choruses that were sung, and which spoke to me powerfully of the Love that will not let me go.

Many of Lorna's friends attended her funeral as also did the small community in support and acknowledgment of our family and friends in their loss. The showering of condolences from the crowds together with words of blessings and shared pain was truly overwhelming and emotional. I had shared with Morag the words that came to me and wanted them declared at the service as a witness to God's love that is stronger than death and felt an urgency that I should read them. She agreed and promised to support me if I was not able to do this when the time came. Remembering God's promises and standing on His word, I did read them and with conviction. My siblings had hired a minibus to travel to Lorna's funeral in Scotland. I accompanied them on the return journey to Wales. How did we spend our time on this long journey? We sang together.

Chapter 23
Welsh Mountain Goats

"Come, let us go up to the mountain[s] of the Lord, to the temple of the God of Jacob. He will teach us His ways, so that we may walk in His paths"
(Micah 4:2).

In the Bible, mountains are mentioned five hundred and seventy times and valleys are mentioned twenty-eight times. Life is a series of mountains and valleys. Each day brings new experiences. Some days are rife with struggles and some are plentiful in joy. Other days are a mixture of both.

From a very early age I've been drawn to hills and mountains – the steeper the better. The farm where my siblings and I grew up was set in a hollow, so we were surrounded by hills. Not a day went by that I didn't climb one of them; always to the summit. As children we would use the wheelbase of the old pram as a toboggan and scurry down the hill using our feet as brakes. It was exhilarating and possibly dangerous but the joy for me would be the climb, anticipating the view from the top before the actual descent which was always over much too quickly.

Among many walking and climbing holidays that I've enjoyed is one that Mair, my Welsh walking buddy and I did in North Wales along with some American tourists and an English guide. Our leader had some difficulty pronouncing "Carneddau" and "Yr Wyddfa" and so Mair and I were called upon to interpret. As a group, we blended well with each other and in time we were referred to as "the two Welsh mountain goats." We were fit in those days and silly too! From the summit of Yr Wyddfa we were blessed with a beautiful sunny day and got a clear view of Llanddwyn Island, the magical part of Anglesey that we had visited the previous day. A rare occurrence.

Mair and I had another unforgettable adventure hiking through the inner Bright Angel and South Kaibab trails to get to the bottom of the Grand Canyon and discovered that summer is not the best time for hiking this distance of sixteen and a half miles round trip. However, it took around eleven hours with the descent and the climb equally exhilarating and tiring.

Yet another memorable climb was Mount Kinabalu in Borneo. This time, being a little older, I was referred to as "Supergran" after completing the four thousand and ninety-five metre climb in two days, along with five young fit Brits. For me it was a return to fitness and what I considered to be an accomplishment following a course of chemotherapy and radiotherapy. What an amazing scene from the top.

Nearer home, completing the Mary Jones walk is one that every Welsh person needs to experience. Having walked the trail on two separate occasions, the scenery is magnificent at any time of year. The story of Mary Jones is well known throughout Wales. Such was her desire to own her very own Bible in Welsh that she walked twenty-six miles to Bala to meet with Reverend Thomas Charles who had promised to get her one. He in turn realised that there was a great need to publish more Bibles in the Welsh language. The British and Foreign Bible Society was formed in 1804 to provide not only Welsh language Bibles, but in other languages throughout the world.

My walking companion this time was Joyce Nuttall together with our guide and friend Mary Thomas from Llanuwchlyn who had recently surveyed and mapped out the route. Who better to guide us than Mary who knew the area so well! She did the local landmarks and the story that led Mary Jones to desire her own Bible. As we rambled, reminisced and talked along the way, we were aware that this walk was history in the making and Joyce and I were pioneers. When the time came to repeat this walk, on this occasion with Beryl our dear friend from NovaScotia, Mair and I thought we would be familiar with the route but alas, it was a different season of the year when spring was in the air. We distinctly heard the cuckoo's call and nature was alive with the sound of its springing. I recall my feet got wet when my boots leaked but I didn't attempt to walk barefooted.

Before this walk, I was visiting a family from Ghana, now living in London, whom I befriended as part of my role with Christian Care, a charity that supports families in need in the Borough of Merton. The family is one that I've supported through some difficult times in their lives, hence we know each other well and I often feel that I am the one that is blessed through their visits. During our chats, I mentioned that I would be away the following week. They were most interested to hear that I was going to walk the Mary Jones trail. "How do you know about Mary Jones?" I asked them. "Of course, I know her story," said the mum of the family. "We were presented with a New Testament in our language at our school and on the front cover was the story of this fifteen-year-old Welsh girl who was prepared to walk barefoot to get her own Bible."

This walk was of such historical importance in 1799 at the time that Mary accomplished this, and it was a privilege to have taken part in it. I am immensely proud to be Welsh, even a Welsh mountain goat.

When summarising walks of life, surely the most precious memories are the long walks over the mountains or in the valleys with family members, alone, or as a prayer walk. Not only is one in touch with nature and fresh air, but it is also often the time to clear the mind of worries, exercise the lungs or have intimate family discussions. Whether we have a mountain top experience or not, I can sometimes identify with Meredith Wilson who coined the song;

There were bells on a hill

But I never heard them ringing,

No, I never heard them at all

'Til there was you!

Yes, there were bells — bluebells! I heard them ringing in the nature chorus and then there was God — the Creator. Yes, I think that every mountain top experience we have energises us so that we are equipped to face the dark valley below.

Chapter 24
Healing Ministry

The Presbyterian Church of Wales' Healing Ministry is based on the belief that Jesus loves and understands every one of us. When we turn to Him, He will listen and respond, using our various gifts as a means to heal others.

In 1954, the Presbyterian Church of Wales established a movement to encourage understanding and practice of Christian Healing. Since then, many people have been involved, both receiving and contributing. At the same time, interest in Christian Healing was on the rise in other branches of the Church and today, many churches throughout the world have accepted this ministry as a natural part of their worship and work.

Although healing may not happen as we expect, when we turn to Jesus with our needs and ask Him to enter our situation, He will always meet us there and will never leave us. Every part of our lives is affected by the healing ministry. It affects our relationship with God, with others, with ourselves and with the world created around us. It works in harmony with the medical profession, nurses and others involved in healing and acknowledges that God uses many means of healing us. The Healing Ministry warns against spiritualism and the harmful influence of the occult. It concerns the whole person: body, mind and spirit. It brings peace and harmony to a needy world.

The apostles returned to Jesus from their ministry tour and told Him all they had done and taught.

Then Jesus said, "Let's go off by ourselves to a quiet place and rest awhile."

This verse comprises for me the need to come away from the busyness of life: to tell, relate and review all that our ministry entails to Jesus as well as the need for solitude, rest and refreshment for ourselves. The annual Ministry of Healing Summer School held in Cefn Lea, Newtown, is the highlight of my summer. Often, not until I "come away to a quiet place" and meet up with others in similar ministries do I realise how exhausted I can become. This is an opportunity for receiving, to be refreshed in body, mind and spirit, and to hear what God is saying in solitude.

There is always joy and laughter on the first day as we assemble into our discussion groups, meeting old friends as well as newcomers to share our stories. At the opening service, there is an opportunity to remember those who in the past year have been promoted to glory. There are moving tributes from those who have been involved in the ministry from its early days and who have witnessed the miraculous healing hand of God in their own lives. One year the theme of the opening service centred on the healing of the paralysed man (Mark 2:1–12). How often we were challenged. Are we, like the four men, moved to compassionate action on behalf of others who have no voice, or those in need of healing? Sometimes, to our shame, we are too busy with our agendas to notice those in our congregations who are hurting.

Each morning we come together for devotions before breakfast, and I was privileged to lead one of these sessions. Surrounded as we were by such magnificent scenery of the Mongomeryshire countryside (my homeland), it was conducive for giving thanks to our Creator God, seeking His direction in our lives as we spend times of quiet reflection thereby equipping us to minister to a needy world. Having two free afternoons afforded time for solitude, prayer or going for a walk and there was time for all three.

In one of the Bible studies, we looked at the healing of Peter's mother-in-law (Matt 8:14–17). During the study, we were asked to imagine ourselves as one of the characters. Interestingly I had no problem identifying with Peter's concern, or with Andrew, James, John and others who were accompanying Jesus and being witnesses of the healing. However, I did not want to be Peter's mother-in-law lying in bed and feeling rotten. Ouch! From conversations with others with medical backgrounds, many feel the same and want to be the one who serves rather than the one receiving.

There was an opportunity for receiving at the blessing service which included prayer, the laying of hands, or anointing with oil. Many of our friends in leadership roles who cannot afford to get time to attend the whole conference, often don't want to miss this blessing service and benefit greatly from being there. The presence of the Spirit is tangible in the stillness and the responsive singing as only the Welsh can sing, in unending praise and worship.

As in previous years, the time of sharing is an extension of the blessing service with many expressing the real thoughts and desires of their hearts in a safe environment. Those who came for the first time said they didn't want to leave and would be back next year. There were harrowing personal stories from Christian leaders in our group who had been through dark times, others falsely accused, struggling with addictions, depression and other mental illnesses. Hearing the honesty and vulnerability of these friends was akin to the stories of persecution that many Christians suffer in different parts of the world. But this is in Britain. How we need to be praying for our leaders and those in the front line who are under severe attack from the enemy!

Before leaving the conference, we came together at the Lord's table to be fed by Him in our hearts by faith with thanksgiving, remembering His ultimate sacrifice on the cross and to remember that we make up the Body of Christ. As part of the Body, we need to be in tune with God in the inevitable busyness that awaits us when we return. May we be obedient to His call to be channels of His grace and healing – the healing that is nourishing for the soul.

With George Matheson's words of his hymn resounding in my ears:

"O Love that will not let me go,

I rest my weary soul in Thee;

I give Thee back the life I owe,

That in Thine ocean depths its flow

May richer, fuller be."

I felt richer for having been fed with Christ's presence and being one with the fellowship of believers, feasted on His love by spending time in solitude, and had my soul nourished and my body refreshed to serve.

If you hear Jesus saying, "Let us go by ourselves to a quiet place and rest awhile", it's worth heeding His voice.

GWEN WILDMAN

Chapter 25
Ffald-y-Brenin and Taizé

For rest, refreshment and restoration, Ffald-y-Brenin is the place to experience the sweetness of God's presence – whether it's for a day, a weekend, or for a longer period. Taizé, for me, is a routine of meeting together to slow down and meditate on Scripture in times of silence.

After reading Roy Godwin's book, 'Grace Outpouring', visiting Ffald-y-Brenin was high on my bucket list. The book is a captivating account of spiritual renewal on a Welsh hillside where God has drawn thousands of seekers to this converted hill farm with a tangible presence of healing and power. My friends from Canada, Stephanie and Carole, had also read the book and were intent on visiting this, by now well-known, house of prayer in the Gwaen Valley. I seized the opportunity to visit this part of Pembrokeshire that was not familiar to me but was popular with tourists. I arranged a week off work and made the booking.

When I went to collect Stephanie and Carol from Heathrow Airport, I hadn't expected Stephanie to be in a wheelchair. During the flight from St John's Newfoundland, she had a flare-up of her Rheumatoid Arthritis symptoms resulting in extreme stiffness of her joints. Within a few days of rest, then some sightseeing in London, a walk in the park and to the shops, the symptoms lessened. I learned from Steph that she had been hospitalised for seven months before her diagnosis of RA with many more months of being wheelchair-bound and receiving rehabilitation to follow. She was anticipating a time of refreshment and healing at Ffald-y-Brenin.

Carol and I had spent time in Wales before, when a group of us from Ireland, Isle of Mann and England had a Grenfell get-together and stayed in Porthgain. We had many a long walk along the coastal hills. This time, Carol had some challenging health needs but wanted to take in the atmosphere of this special place most of all. A friend of mine from my local church, whom I had invited to make up the foursome, could not get the time off at the last minute. I was delighted when Hazel from our Taizé group agreed to come with us. Looking back, as we gelled together and shared incidences as a group, this was definitely God-ordained.

Whether joining various activity groups, attending services in the chapel four times a day, sitting quietly, reading, strolling the grounds or hiking the hills, and reflecting on the ancient paths, it was all soul nourishment. Not to be missed was a stroll to the high cross said to have magnetic powers where individuals or groups would gather to worship or just to gaze. On our last night we asked Steph, as an ordained United Church of Canada minister, if she would like to administer communion to us in the intimacy of the chapel. She was unsure about handling the elements when her finger joints were swollen with limited movements, but she went away to spend some time in prayer before deciding. Meanwhile we took the liberty of asking fellow guests to join us as we were due to leave the following day. The chapel, hewn into the rock, seats twelve people comfortably and on this special night it was almost full, and Steph led us in a moving communion service managing the bread and wine without a tremor. A sure sign that the Spirit was tangible as no one wanted to leave. A true healing.

Taizé is a monastic community in France, founded in the 1940s by a Swiss named Roger Louis Schütz-Marsauche known as Brother Roger. I have been drawn to Taizé's contemplative form of worship and its emphasis on ecumenism since I joined our local group. After an exhausting and stressful day at work, I didn't always have the energy or feel like going out but, it was refreshing to meet together and share our joys and concerns. I particularly like the meditative singing, the liturgical readings and the period of silence before open prayer. Sharing our concerns for the world and each other is healing and, for me, therapeutic.

GWEN WILDMAN

Chapter 26
Retirement and Christian CARE Merton

"You are never too old to set another goal or to dream a new dream."
– C.S. Lewis

I had mentally started to prepare and wind down my working hours several years before my retirement date. Among the top tips we are advised to think about is to get our finances in order first. However, top of my list was to give my services and expertise back to the community. Long before I retired from work, I was involved with Christian CARE Merton – a local charity supporting families who live in poverty. Christian CARE was founded in 1967 by Bert Hyde following an ecumenical Lent group who were discussing homelessness at the time and were inspired by the Bible story of the Good Samaritan. One of the group members discovered a dwelling in the area that was housing those seeking asylum and alerted Merton council to action help for them. I have befriended several families over the past twenty-five years, and it's been a real privilege especially when a firm trust is formed between us. From my initial visit when the families are at their lowest ebb and in great need, to seeing them get on their feet and established in a job, it is great being part of the ups and downs of their lives and sharing their dreams. It's never too late to pursue a new passion and for me, Street Pastors is my great passion.

GWEN WILDMAN

Chapter 27
Street Pastors

I've often been challenged, following a wonderful uplifting church service where I received and worshiped but not participated, to "now go and do it!" I'm reminded of the words of Dr Martin Lloyd-Jones when he quoted that "mere theoretical Christianity is useless." Some Christians owe allegiance to their denominations or traditions or structure. Street Pastors is the church on the street.

When worshipping at the Methodist church, I recite this Covenant prayer at the beginning of each year, and I am often challenged by the second line of the prayer which says:

Put me to what You will,

rank me with whom You will.

I became a Street Pastor in 2010 and it is such a privilege and a pleasure to be ranked with Christians of other denominations, theology and backgrounds when patrolling the streets. We can have different and diverse ways of sharing our faith, but we are united and are "all one in Christ Jesus." Some of the people we meet on the streets seem surprised that we are from different churches and come together as the "Church on the Streets." They also express surprise when asked why we are doing this, that we are volunteers!

I volunteered to join a Street Pastor team one night as an Observer, the main reason being to introduce my friend

Margaret from Kenya who was staying with me at the time to experience how the churches in Britain was responding to problems of the young. Margaret was keen to set up a program to help those with drug dependency in and around Nairobi. On that first night outside a night club in Wimbledon, a young, distressed lady came out and fell into my arms pouring out her story. She had recently had a termination of pregnancy and after a few drinks realised that she had not dealt with the loss. What a privilege to be able to listen to her and to direct her to the professional help that she needed.

We are often referred to as "angels." Angels are God's messengers – they patrol the earth, protect the helpless and offer encouragement. Street Pastors also proclaim God's messages especially when giving out flip-flops, wristbands, lollipops or water. I'm especially proud to wear my Street Pastor jacket because it has the Welsh words written on it "Bugeiliad y Stryd" and that translated to English is Street Shepherds and that, I think, is what we are.

Working together with other Christians from other denominations and all sharing God's compassion for those we meet on the streets is a tremendous blessing. The sharing of skills is a blessing that God uses. For example, one of our Street Pastors used to be a rough sleeper for many years. It was the Street Pastors that befriended him, introduced him to the helping agencies and rehabilitation centres. He started going to church and became a Christian. Contacts from the church helped him sort out his immigration documents, so that he eventually got on his feet, got a job and completed his Street Pastor training. What a great asset he is to the team!

At the beginning of this year, we patrolled in Wimbledon. The clubs seemed empty but there were lots of young people outside in groups maybe because the weather was mild. Before the start, I remember that we prayed for epiphany moments, but nothing dramatic happened. We had our break at the Alex pub, the manager Sam was delighted to see us and made us a cup of tea as he usually does. His beaming smile was the epiphany moment.

There are too many highlights to record when out on patrol and no two nights are the same. One evening I was patrolling with a very experienced team and team leader. There was a group of young men congregating together some of whom looked, to me, a bit menacing. Normally, if I were to encounter them on my path, even if I'm with others, I would probably avoid them altogether. This team leader who is always up for a challenge walked straight up to them, greeted them by shaking hands and blesses them. Suddenly I could see the change in their attitude and gradually smiles appeared on their faces. The rest of the team including myself followed suit and the young people welcomed us. One of them said, "I do like to be blessed."

Street Pastors are blessed by God to be a blessing to others.

GWEN WILDMAN

Chapter 28
Open the Book

Jesus said, "Let the children come to me, and do not hinder them, for the kingdom of heaven belongs to such as these."
– Matthew 19:14

Most of the activities I've taken up since retirement are working with different denominations and enjoying the things that unite us as Christians. In recent years it has been an absolute privilege to be part of the Open the Book Bible Society team in the Borough of Merton. I fortunately joined at a time when the team was already well established and had a store of storytelling costumes and visual aids at hand in one of the local churches. Open the Book is a fantastic opportunity to introduce primary school stories from Bob Hartman's Storyteller Bible and to dramatise these in their school's Collective Worship.

During the pandemic when we could no longer visit schools, our team continued to meet regularly via Zoom for prayer and support. Before long the technophile members of the team devised a method to video record the sessions every week and these were shared with other teams online with the hope that the schools would use these videos when the schools reopened. We soon learned a lot about green screens and background effects.

We currently have an enthusiastic team of nine volunteers from four different churches and meet initially to pray, rehearse and gather the appropriate props needed for the particular story. Most of the work is in the preparation and I've learned that you don't have to be a budding actor or actress, but just a heart to share Bible stories to young children, some of whom would never get to hear these stories from any other source.

What joy when you receive the highest accolade from a child who, on recognising you will call out, "You're Jesus!"

Chapter 29
World Day of Prayer

I have seen many eye-catching church wall hangings, appliques and signs with the words, "Prayer Changes Things" inscribed in bold print as if to highlight this.

For many years, I have been involved with the World Day of Prayer movement, formerly "Women's World Day of Prayer." It is a women-led, global and largest ecumenical movement in the world.

It started with dedicated Christian women who were practical and praying for the needs of the world, especially for women and children in the mission field. From the start, the women agreed that prayer should be informed and lead to prayerful action.

The motto of the World Day of Prayer movement is "Informed Prayer and Prayerful Action." Through their participation in the World Day of Prayer, it affirms that prayer and action are inseparable and that both have immeasurable influence on the world. The National Committee of World Day of Prayer, England, Wales and Northern Ireland can award many grants each year to Registered Christian Charities, to assist their projects throughout the world, especially in the writer-country of the year of request.

Since living in London, I have been involved with the WDP services at the local level, but it was when I joined the WDP National Committee that I learned more about this prayer movement. The movement is an apt description, for it is never still and it is not just a one-day-a-year event on the first Friday of March. Having now spent four years on the National Committee representing the Welsh-Speaking churches, I am in awe of the amount of prayer work, travelling for preparation days, meetings and fundraising done by these dedicated women. It cannot be measured. It was an exceptional privilege to be representing the Welsh churches in Wales and London and once again being able to worship and sing in my native tongue.

I was also fortunate to be invited to the WDP International Committee in 2022 where one hundred and eighty-seven representatives from one hundred and three countries were participating via Zoom in the opening service for the three-day meeting which was hosted by Scotland. Imagine my surprise and delight to see Reverend Steph McClellan's smiling face on the screen! Steph was elected a Caribbean and North America representative of the executive group for the WDPIC. What a privilege and what a joy to have "met" again.

Prayer does change things.

Chapter 30
God of Restoration

The basis of my faith and hope in this life is a belief in a God of restoration. This is fundamental to my faith as a Christian. Even when I have strayed from His pathway, with repentance I will be reinstated to a place of blessing. By faith, I am reconciled to God and my relationship with Him is restored forever. My life journey has not been a rags-to-riches story; rather, I have learned to take care of myself and my family through the skint years. The rewards are not monetary, but I'm now full of thankfulness and joy to have a restored relationship with my children.

Heidi works as a children's doctor but writes fiction in her spare time. Tanya is a Senior Scientist in chemistry, Design and Analysis. My son-in-law is area vice president of a software firm. They have illustrious careers, but to me they are precious children

We Kept a Welcome in the Hillside

When Francis (now called John) and I celebrated our sixtieth birthday, we had the opportunity to go back to Gorsdyfwch and have a family reunion with a difference. We sought permission from the landowner for by this time the house was derelict and boarded up, used only for animal shelter and tending to the sheep. Where during our childhood there was a mountain pass, there is now an unclassified road. This would be music to Dad's ears! The hillside area has not lost its beauty. What we used to perceive as desolate is now a paradise. The weather was glorious, the skies blue, the sunrise and sunset equally magical. In the evenings the singing got better and the storytelling longer. The air seemed unpolluted until we arrived in cars. Despite our attempts to get back to nature, we found it would have been impossible to come without transport, to carry generators for the fridge, the barbecue and bottled water.

Gorsdyfwch House

Fast forward to another decade, the now extended family gathered together again at Gorsdyfwch. This time, my grandchildren – Holly, Esther and Scott – were fascinated with the whole experience. How was it ever possible to survive without Wi-Fi connection? they asked. No way could they survive without their iPads. The journey was different in that there were wind turbines on the horizon and no entry signs to the areas where underground cables were being laid for wind farms. On the journey in the car, Holly was baffled by my collection of audiotape cassettes. She picked one up and asked me what it was! It hadn't occurred to me that, of course, this was all unfamiliar to my grandchildren.

I couldn't help comparing the huge gap in the generational way of living. Whereas we had our local postman deliver our letters as one method of communication, my grandchildren could watch movies on their iPads and talk to their friends on their mobile phones. To our generation, "Kindles" was a kindle of kittens, or some small combustible bits of wood collected to start a fire. Or, if we wanted to make up a song as we were wont to do, Charles Wesley's resounding words, "Kindle a Flame of Sacred Love", would be very fitting to sing, once the barbecue was lit.

My childhood was not all toil. My siblings and I made up imaginative stories, acted on them, played at eisteddfods and concerts, and made up tanks and tractors out of cotton reels. The haystack and the granary provided good safe places for hide-and-seek games. In the summer holidays, the older siblings would organise our own sports day with races and high jumps. It became very competitive until the younger siblings got tired. Then the older ones would let them win a race or two.

GWEN WILDMAN

Conclusion

I bumped into Jen, a work colleague, shortly after I retired. We had not seen each other for many years. It was a busy Saturday morning just before Christmas and a group of us were singing Christmas Carols in Wimbledon Centre Court shopping centre. Just a week later, we met again. Twice in one week! This time, I was rattling a collection tin outside the shopping centre, fundraising for a local charity. Jen greeted me with an exclamation, "Gwen! Don't you ever do anything normal?" That remark got me thinking, especially as my Canadian friends would comment that I was possibly abnormal for getting a buzz out of flying low in a twin-engine Cessna plane in Labrador! What I consider to be entirely normal is decidedly off-key for some and certainly not shared by some of today's standards. As we were reminded during this writing course, we are all wired differently.

As I consider how God has designed and placed me at this point in history, he has also placed passions and more callings on my heart which I would like to pursue. Colours are an important part of our lives, adding excitement and vibrancy. I have been blessed with a colourful past, but not in shocking terms. To quote C. S. Lewis, "We must show our Christian colours if we are to be true to Jesus Christ." Whether it's the blue rinse for the washing, my green Crosville coat or my red plastic bucket on the beach – I'm seeing life with new eyes from God's perspective.

My prayer

God, You are worthy of all my praise and You created me to praise You.

Please show me how to worship You in all that I do. When people look back on my life, I want them to give You glory. So please teach me how to make my life an act of worship. In Jesus' name, Amen.

About the Author

Gwen Wildman (née Jones) lives in South London and is a retired nurse, mother of three and has three grandchildren. She is currently Secretary of the Welsh Presbyterian Church in Sutton where she worships in her native language. She is passionate about music, gardening, hiking, cross-stitch and Sudoku.

GWEN WILDMAN

References

Dr. Enoch, D. 2022. 'Enoch's Walk, Ninety-Five, Not Out: Journey of a Psychiatrist. Published by: Y. Lolfa.

Evans, D. M. 2003. "A District Nurse in Rural Wales Before the National Health Service." Publisher Gwasg Carreg Gwalch.

Godwin, R. 2012. "The Grace Outpouring." Dave Roberts was published by David C Cook.

Levenston, M. 'The Pig Man and Pig Bins of WWII'. *Royal Voluntary Service.* [Online]. Available at: https://suttoninashfield.wixsite.com/sutton-in-ashfield/story-03 (Accessed at: 3 June 2024).

Presbyterian Church of Wales. [Online]. Available at: https://www.ebcpcw.cymru/cy/

Vaughan-Thomas, W. "Madly in All Directions." 1967. Publishers Longmans, Green and Co Ltd.

Christian CARE is a charity working in the London Borough of Merton, committed to the relief of poverty within Merton. There are a group of sixty volunteers, many from churches of different denominations across Merton, who show care and concern for our neighbours as Jesus did. In 2017 Christian CARE Merton was awarded the Queen's Award for Voluntary Service.

Merton Street Pastors is a group of ordinary Christians from local churches in Merton, motivated by the love of Jesus. They go out late on Friday nights to patrol the streets of Mitcham since 2005, Wimbledon since 2009 and Morden from 2026; looking to care for people, to listen to people and help people. In 2024 Merton Street Pastors were thrilled to be awarded the Queen's Award for Voluntary Service.

About PublishU

PublishU is transforming the world of publishing.

PublishU has developed a new and unique approach to publishing books, offering a three-step guided journey to becoming a globally published author!

We enable hundreds of people a year to write their book within 100-days, publish their book in 100-days and launch their book over 100-days to impact tens of thousands of people worldwide.

The journey is transformative, one author said,

"I never thought I would be able to write a book, let alone in 100 days... now I'm asking myself what else have I told myself that can't be done that actually can?'"

To find out more visit
www.PublishU.com

GWEN WILDMAN

Printed in Great Britain
by Amazon